1

5

Terry's book, *What c*  cowboy, young or old. It's] brand of humor. *What a R*
Even though Terry I.
Rodeo, he was a very successful bull rider. National Finals Rodeo qualifications don't justify or quantify a bull riding career nor should it! I trust Terry totally for his expertise in bull riding instruction. He's a great role model and prayer warrior. The Holland's are a wonderful family who love the Lord Jesus and live life to its fullest.

While reading the book, I found myself with sweaty palms and that feeling only bull riders know. I was continually amazed at how accurately Terry describes all the emotions that occur while anticipating and executing a ride—fear, joy, excitement. Wow! Do yourself a favor and give it a read—you won't be disappointed.

Don Gay—Eight time PRCA World Champion Bull Rider, 1974, 1975, 1976, 1977, 1979, 1980, 1981, and 1984.

* * *

Terry Holland and I have been friends since 1985. I admire him for his love and faithfulness to Debbie Jo. His life is an example to his daughter Khakie, of what godly manhood looks like.

Besides being a great bull rider, he has always had an extraordinary gift for telling a story. Terry has told stories that have made my sides hurt from laughter as well as stories about his relationship with God and compassion for people that have brought tears to my eyes.

Reading through the pages of *What A Ride!* stirred up in me the very reason I felt so passionate about riding bulls and reminded me of what has kept me so close to the sport. Many people's lives have been affected because of having Terry a part in them. Terry is a shining example of what Jesus meant when he said in John 15:8, "This is to my Father's glory, that you bear much fruit, showing yourselves to be my disciples."

Enjoy reading *What A Ride!* and you'll understand why thousands of men have followed the dream of riding bulls.

Cody Custer—PRCA World Champion Bull Rider, 1992

What a Ride!

Terry Holland
with
Nanci G. Huyser

To Mark + Deb,

Keep Your Eyes on Jesus!
Keep up the good work,
Thanks for all you do
for our Lord.

Terry
Holland

903.754.2619

What a Ride!

Terry Holland
with
Nanci G. Huyser

Buoy Up
Press

Denton Texas

Cover photo by Al Long, Granbury, Texas

Buoy Up Press
An imprint of AWOC.COM Publishing
P.O. Box 2819
Denton, TX 76202

Manufactured in the United States of America

ISBN: 978-0-937660-14-0

What A Ride! is dedicated to my father, Leland Holland. In eighty-four years he never drank or smoked and none of his three sons ever heard him say a cuss word. He survived the Depression, but he never turned loose of the principles he learned from it. He loved one woman for sixty-six years. My brothers and I are the men we have become because of Daddy. Thanks "Big L."

Chapter 1

I fell in love with riding bulls when I was a little bitty boy. I love them. I love the way they smell. I love the way they think and react. I study them. I just *love* bulls.

My daddy was chairman of the rodeo committee in Carthage, Texas, when I was about five. I went to the rodeo office and arena with him a lot, which exposed me to rodeo at a young age. I was with my dad one day when Jim Shoulders came to town.

I'd say Jim's the greatest cowboy who ever lived—absolutely a legend. He won sixteen world championships in professional rodeo, and held the record of seven world championships in bull riding until Donnie Gay broke his record. At the time, Jim wasn't competing in rodeo anymore. He worked as a livestock contractor and raised *great* bulls. He's always been kind of famous because he does public relations work and rodeo appearances.

I remember meeting Jim at the rodeo office when it was in Joe's Café. "This is my boy, Terry," Dad said, grinning at the other men standing around who were as enamored as I was with this rodeo hero.

Jim and I shook hands—his calloused and large, mine little-boy small. Then he said, "Terry, you want me to sign you up in the bull riding?"

"Yeah, I mean, *yes sir!*" I could hardly speak. I sure did!

Everybody laughed, and well, that shook me up.

As time went on people began asking me, "Terry, what are you going do when you grow up?"

I couldn't get it out of my mind. "I'm gonna be a bull rider. I want to be *just* like Jim Shoulders."

That became my focus and goal in life. I never wavered, even though my mother did her best to change my mind and thinking.

My daddy took me along to the rodeo arena. I watched the livestock unload off the trucks. Man, I'd stare at those bucking bulls and watch them come down the ramp. I loved seeing old Andy Capp, Mighty Mouse, The Grim Reaper, Dr. Jekyll, and Mr. Hyde, Batman, Robin, and all the other great bulls.

From the time I was six years old, I studied bulls and watched them buck at the rodeo. They develop tendencies of moving the same way every time they're ridden, and I was familiar with each bull's pattern. I knew how they bucked better than the cowboys. I had paid attention to them the year before at the local rodeo and watched them eat, drink, sleep, lay down, and get up. I knew their habits and how they behaved.

Cowboys who came to town for the rodeos were scared because Jim Shoulders' bulls were so bad, "rank," as we call them in rodeo. They were tough to stay on. So, the cowboys tried to come up with a game plan. A lot of them didn't know the bulls, but they'd heard about a kid in town who did, so they'd come find me.

"Are you the little boy around here who knows more about the bulls than we do?" one cowboy asked.

I adjusted my hat and looked up at him. "Yeah, I know 'em. Which one did ya get?"

"Well, what's ol' Andy Capp doing?"

"Andy Capp's a chopped-off-horned-tiger-striped brindle bull. He's gonna turn back to the left, right at the gate. *If you're still on him after about four seconds, which you won't be, he'll reverse and spin.*" I knew 'em all right.

During the rodeo while the bulls waited in the chutes as the cowboys strapped on their ropes, I'd sneak up and pluck a bit of hair off each bull. One at a time, I saved the hair in a little jar and stuck a piece of masking tape on it. I wrote that bull's number and name on his jar of hair. After about three years, I had between thirty to forty bottles. I think it's probably the greatest collection of bucking bull hair that's ever been assembled.

I had a friend who went to Chicago to see a baseball game. He came back with a little bottle of dirt off the mound at Wrigley Field. He thought it was pretty cool.

"Let me show you what I've got," I told him. After I showed him my collection of bucking bull hair, he wanted to trade me his dirt for five bottles of hair, which I didn't do. Like I said, I love bulls. I even have that bull hair to prove it!

Jim Shoulders had a notorious, bad-as-there-ever-was bull named Big Bad John—a huge tiger-striped bull that cowboys claimed to be the best they'd ever ridden. And I wanted to ride him.

I was about eight when I started hounding my dad. "Daddy, I'm gonna be a bull rider. I can ride one of Jim Shoulders' bulls. You're his friend. Please let me ride one. Ask Jim Shoulders. Beg him if you have to, but please, set it up." I had faith; I *knew* I could do it.

Daddy looked at me like I was crazy. "Son, when you're grown you can do anything you want to do. If it's riding bulls, then you get after it but until you're grown, you ain't ridin' bulls."

It broke my heart, but I honored my daddy and I waited, and waited, and waited. Finally, I was grown. At least I thought so. I must have been about ten. We were working calves at the ranch one spring afternoon and had about a hundred cows in the corral and the herd bulls in a pen. My favorite smells lingered in the air—cattle and manure.

I sidled up to daddy. "First things first, Mother's gone to town and we've got the bulls up."

He nodded. I'm sure he knew what was coming next.

I pointed toward the pen. "Let me ride one of these ol' boys. I know they ain't rodeo bulls; they're herd bulls. But they're still bulls. We've got the side delivery gates just like at the rodeo arena. Let me ride one! Please?" It wasn't set up as a bucking chute but it was fixing to work real good anyhow.

"Terry. You're a little boy." Daddy took off his cap and ran his fingers through his hair. "Those bulls weigh eighteen-hundred to nineteen-hundred pounds. I can't let you ride one."

I hooked my thumbs through the belt loops of my Wranglers. "Well, then let me ride a cow. I ain't picky." Not picky, just desperate.

"Our cows weigh twelve to thirteen hundred pounds. I can't let you ride one of them either."

We'd just finished working a little 350-pound Simmental cross-bred heifer calf, and she still stood in the chute. We'd ear tagged her, cut a notch in her ear, wormed, and vaccinated her with two or three different vaccines. A bad day for a calf. She was all stirred up.

My daddy looked at me, at the heifer, then back at me. "Tell you what, we're going to get this out of your system *right* now. You get a rope and get it on this heifer calf," he said. "We're fixin' to bull ride."

My hands get sweaty now just thinking about it. I looked around and found a half-rotten lead rope off an old horse halter. I tied a knot in the end and made a loop in it so I could put it around the heifer like I'd seen the bull riders do. I knew how they put those ropes on the bulls and even though this wasn't a bull rope, this was *my* chance and I wasn't about to miss it.

I grabbed that rope and threw it on her right quick, before my daddy had a chance to change his mind. Daddy took a stick, reached through the chute under the heifer to catch the end of the rope, pulled it up to me, and I got it around her. She squirmed all over that chute, bumping the wooden slat sides. I sat down on her just like I'd seen those bull riders do. I'd been waiting for this chance my whole life.

I sat there thinking. *This ain't even a bull calf. It's a little heifer. Well, this little girl calf's daddy was a bull and that's good enough right now. I'm not gonna blow my chance on a technicality.* I pulled the rope as tight as I thought it should be. It started making funny sounds like it might break, so I decided that was good enough. I scooted up on the rope, got a good grip, and knew what to say. Back in the old days, the cowboys yelled "outside" when they were ready for the bull to be released into the arena. This was my moment. I swallowed once, and as loud as I could muster I hollered, "Outside."

Chapter 2

Daddy swung the old wooden gate. "Eeeeeeeeeee," it creaked and we were free.

That little hussy went "braaaahhhh!" She jumped as high as my daddy's head. She wadded me up and chunked me out in the pen. To tell you how long I rode her, well, I hit the ground before she did.

My mouth wide open and only half-done saying, "outside," still working on "...side," I hit the ground so hard it knocked the breath out of me. I scooped me up a face full of fresh... well, we'd run about a hundred cows through there that particular day, so you can imagine what I got up my nose and in my mouth.

I lay in the corral groaning and thought I was about to die. My dad came running—she'd tossed me way out there. Looking back, I know his life flashed before his eyes. He at least wondered where he'd be sleeping for the next couple of weeks if something has happened to his baby boy. I couldn't talk, just grunted and moaned.

He surveyed the situation, not knowing what to do. Finally, he undid my britches, grabbed me by my little no-longer-white T-shirt, yanked me upright, and pulled my face right up close. "Son! Son! Are you all right?"

I got a little air, spit out some of that stuff, and finally got to where I could grin and talk. "Daddy, that's the most fun I've ever had in my life."

At our ranch, we didn't have any crossbred bulls like those used for bucking in rodeos. We just had fat, gentle bulls, but they were bulls and I had some practicing to do. I couldn't work on my skills just any time. I had to wait until my folks weren't home.

Mother went to the beauty shop and still does. She's got a different day now, but back then her appointment was every Friday at four o'clock. Daddy went to town every

Friday afternoon to pay his carpenters. In addition to ranching, he was a building contractor.

You could bet on it—Fridays at four was obviously the best time for me to practice bull riding. My brother and I always had a bunch of friends over on Friday afternoons, rain or shine. By having a baseball game in progress, we made it look real good.

My little heart started beating faster whenever my dad left in his pick up, and I saw my mother crank up that old 1965 Galaxy 500 Ford and back out of the garage. When she hit Highway 79 and as her tail lights disappeared over the last hill right before Crawford Parker's house, everyone ran straight from the baseball field to the corral. It didn't matter if one of us had knocked the ball clear to the neighbor's place, we stopped immediately because they all knew I was going to ride something. It was four on Friday!

We all ran to the corral one afternoon after my mother left and found nothing there but an old Brown Swiss bull. Brown Swiss are not notorious rodeo bulls. They're not really good for our kind of cattle operation. They're just cattle. Why we had him, I don't know, but he was a bull and it was Friday. He stood in the corral, so I obviously had plans for him. We put the Brown Swiss in the chute, and I threw a rope around him while my friends cheered me on.

When I was ready, I hollered, "Outside."

Lonnie and Bill swung the gate open. Nothing happened. The Brown Swiss never even moved. He just stood there. Chewing his cud. If you know anything about cattle, you'd know he was about as relaxed as he could get. He looked like my dad when he'd try to stay up and watch the evening news. This bull seemed like he was about to nod off.

The boys shut the gate and put their heads together.

"My uncle rides bulls at Houston, Terry," one of my friends said. "He uses spurs. You ain't got none. If you put spurs on, he'll buck."

"I know where some are," yelled my brother Tim. Off he ran to the barn and came back with a set of great big old Mexican spurs with huge rowels—those are the little jingly parts that spin around. I slid them on the heels of my boots. I don't know why we had them, but they were fixing to get used.

I climbed back on the Brown Swiss. "Outside," I hollered again. The gate swung open. I dug in my spurs, and man, was my friend ever right. Spurs worked. It felt like the bull jumped plumb across the corral. When he made a drastic cut to the left, I didn't. I kept right on going, slammed into the fence and hit a big crosstie post with my leg.

If I'd gotten injured, I couldn't let my mother know because she'd shut me down. I always said I wasn't going to, but if I did get hurt, I'd be one tough little cowboy. I *had* to be tough. I *couldn't* get hurt.

Well, after my encounter with that fence post, I started to bawl and squall. Before I even hit the ground, it hurt. Bad.

My friends thought they'd save me. They'd seen bull fighters like Jim Hill, who worked for Jim Shoulders in the 1960s, rescue cowboys at the rodeo. They ran in, picked me up, and crammed me through about a six-inch crack in the corral fence. Meanwhile, the Brown Swiss bull walked over and started eating from the feed trough.

"My leg's broken," I wailed. It hurt and wouldn't ease up.

Tim jumped over the fence to where I lay.

I knew fear had him by the throat, because he feared mother as much as I did.

He glared down at me. "What's wrong with you?"

I winced. "I broke my leg."

Tim shook his head. "Nah, you didn't."

"How do you know? You ain't a doctor."

"I know that if you did, Mother's gonna kill me. Your leg is *not* broken. As a matter of fact, you're gonna be playin' baseball at five o'clock when she gets back."

Mother always got back home from the beauty shop about ten after five. The boys dragged me under the barn and stacked some square baled hay around, I guess to hide me, in case things turned out bad.

Sure enough—you can call my brother a prophet if you want to—I was playing baseball with a slight limp at ten minutes after five.

I attended a seminar for ranchers with my daddy one day. I had no idea what the meeting was about and just daydreamed about riding bulls as I sat there.

One of the speakers stood up to talk. "What you ranchers need to do, if you're going to make a little profit from your ranch, is to use some crossbred bulls with your cows."

What did he say? I perked right up and elbowed my daddy. "Did you hear that? Crossbred bulls! We can get some *profit*." I won't lie. I was just a boy and didn't even know what "profit" meant.

"You know, Mother would like some profit, too. Profit, how 'bout that?" Thoughts bucked and spun through my mind. *Somebody's done planted the seed about a crossbred bull in my daddy's head. God, thank you. What a great day!*

Several other speakers made presentations at the seminar, but I could only remember the one about crossbred bulls and profit.

Our conversation on the way home reflected my preoccupation. "Daddy, how 'bout that speaker? Them crossbred bulls, how 'bout it? That's what we need."

Daddy just scratched his head and kept driving.

"Daddy, where do those crossbred bulls come from—those *real* rodeo bulls like we see on TV and at the rodeo?" I asked him more than once. We didn't have any of the "right" kind of bulls on our ranch, and I wanted to know where we could get one.

My daddy, he's the same now as he was then—slow to change. So, absolutely nothing happened.

Well, two or three months went by. One afternoon Tim and I got off the school bus and moseyed up the gravel driveway to the house. The bus cleared our drive and just as it did, my daddy turned in with a gooseneck cattle trailer behind his pickup. He was hauling the most beautiful crossbred bull I'd ever seen in my life. I took one glance at that son-of-a-gun, pitched my school books aside, and took off running. I slid in my tennis shoes right up to the trailer. The bull spun around, slobbering, and stared down at me. I looked right back at him. *This is the greatest thing that's ever happened in my young life.*

Big. Black. Horns sticking out everywhere. He was a bad cat—the real deal.

I remember seeing a leaf float down into the trailer and he pounced on it; hooked it to shreds with those horns of his. That's how bad he was. You didn't dare walk behind him. He'd spin around and stare at you.

"God, I have been praying for a crossbred bull, and you dropped him off right behind the school bus!"

My daddy got out of the truck and walked straight toward me. I never got to say a word. He shook his finger in my face. "Terry. Look at me."

I looked at him.

"Whatever you do, do *not* ride this bull."

Well, I didn't ride him... 'til that next Friday at four o'clock.

Chapter 3

Usually, there were a bunch of boys around to take care of the gate and get the bull up. That day, Tim had taken all the big guys worth any help fishing, of all things.

The day I rode Caesar, my first crossbred bull, only one little boy came to my house. His name was Chuck. He was close to my age, around twelve, but a finicky eater. A little, bitty thing, Chuck weighed about forty-five to fifty pounds. He came down to my house wearing short pants, riding a green Spider bicycle.

Back then, our mothers used clippers on our heads to make it easier to get the ticks off in the summer when we played in the woods. With a burr, they didn't have to dig through a bunch of hair after we came in at night.

Chuck had a burr haircut. Earlier in the day he'd been playing in his mother's flower bed. Sweat trails ran down his dirty, little face. He'd been scratching chigger and tick bites, and little red bumps covered his legs. His waggly sox hung around his ankles. I tell y'all this, because that's all the help I had getting on my first crossbred bull. No way was I going to wait a whole week until the next Friday at four.

We managed to coax the bull into the chute.

"What do you want me to do?" Chuck asked.

I looked at Chuck. Sized him up. It didn't take long to figure out where his value came in. "Chuck, here's what I need you to do. There's a roof on the shed that sticks out over this corral. I need you to stand in front. And whatever you do, do not let this bull buck under the shed's roof. If he gets in there, he could hurt me."

"Well, I'm gonna need a stick or something," Chuck said, shaking his head.

I finally found a stick he could hold up. Chuck went and stood in front of the shed. I climbed into the chute with Caesar. He was the real deal. As I look back across time, he'd be the real deal even now.

I had a little dilemma. With Chuck over by the shed, no one could open the chute. So I ran out to my dad's shop and got a couple of pulleys. I tied a hay string from the latch at the gate, ran it to a pulley at the corner to another pulley half-way down. All I had to do, when I got ready to release this bull to the arena since I didn't have enough help, was pull the string, kick the gate open, and turn him out.

It should work, right?

I sat on Caesar and started to pull the rope up tight around him. I first noticed his back was solid—hard as a rock, and he wasn't even trying. All the bulls I'd been on before were soft, pudgy, and friendly. But this one seemed flexed all the time.

As I pulled the rope, Caesar dropped his head to the ground and dragged a horn up the wooden chute. Splinters flew into the air and on my face. He lowered his head and did it again, trailing the tip of his horn up the side of the old wood-slatted chute. More splinters landed on my ball cap, chest, and in my lap. *Can it get any better than this right here?*

I took a wrap. "Chuck, you ready?"

He gulped. "I'm r-r-ready."

I reached over and pulled the little hay string. "Click," went the latch. "Eeeek." The gate moved a tiny bit.

I took a deep breath. "I'm fixin' to ride me a crossbred bull!" I kicked the gate open.

The best way I know to explain this is, I thought my daddy's bull had blown to pieces. I thought body parts were about to land everywhere. We talk about a bull or horse "blowing up" on you. It felt like he had literally *exploded* underneath me.

"Holy mackerel! I'm in for it now!"

On the second jump, I discovered Caesar was still in one piece. Right about then, I said a quick prayer. *Lord, get me off this thing. Please. Please. I ain't ready for no cross-bred bull!* I didn't have long to say a prayer, but I jumbled it up right quick the best I could.

I accidentally stayed on him for three jumps. I could not believe what he was doing—he spun and bucked at the same time. I didn't know how to ride a spinning bull!

God answered my prayer right away and I was thrown off. Everything except my hand. You've seen it happen in rodeos before. My hand got stuck, hung up in that bull rope.

This ride wasn't like the one up at Walmart where the quarter finally runs out. I couldn't unplug him or shut him off. Caesar kept bucking and seemed to be having fun with me.

It's funny where your thoughts wander in a situation like this. I thought, *There ain't nobody here but Chuck.* And Chuck was doing his best.

"Terry, quit riding him!" Chuck waved his arms and hollered as loud as he could.

By then, my feet and body were nowhere near the bull. I cart-wheeled like a rag doll in the air beside him, still connected by a hand. He stomped. He hooked.

Poor Chuck couldn't take it any longer. "Please Terry! Quit riding him," he screamed, frantic.

Back then bulls scared us plenty, but all the boys I knew, including me, were more afraid of our mothers. Chuck knew if something bad happened and he could be connected to the deal, he'd be in deep trouble.

"Turn loose of him, Terry, and quit riding!" Chuck yelled again.

I *wanted* to quit riding. Really, I did.

Finally, the bull bucked and stomped so hard, so many times, he stepped on me and my hand popped out from the rope. He spun around and backed up, tossed his head in the air and stood there looking down at me.

I evaluated the situation and decided it would be nice if I could stand. I scrambled to my feet and found I had not a shred of shirt left on my body. Somehow the bull stepped right in the back of my britches, broke my belt, and ripped my pants. When I stood, my pants slid down around my ankles.

It was the only time in my career a bull stomped me plumb naked.

"It don't get no better than this," I said, shaking my head at Chuck as I looked around the corral.

"I've got to ride one, too," Chuck said, excitement rising in his voice.

"Now, Chuck, you don't need to get on a real bull," I said. "Get it on your mind, get psyched up. Come on down later, and I'll get you the right calf."

Burying my torn clothes in the pasture crossed my mind, but I didn't have time.

Mom, looking good after her beauty shop appointment, held my jeans and tee shirt at arm's length and gave me a look like only a mother could. About then my daddy walked in. He looked from me to mom, then back at me. "Say son, those baseball games are gettin' mighty rough."

"Yessir, they sure are." I eased through the door back outside and heaved a sigh of relief.

On a Friday afternoon about three weeks later, Chuck rode his Spider bicycle down to my house. He couldn't wear shorts to ride a bull, so he'd put on a pair of long, corduroy pants with elastic in the waist. He was so skinny, he couldn't wear a belt. They didn't make them that small. Chuck skidded to a stop in the yard, a full-sized football helmet dangling from a handlebar.

"What *is* that?" I asked as he jumped off his bike.

"It's a Green Bay Packer helmet. My daddy got it as a souvenir. Man, I can't get hurt. My mother'll kill me." Chuck wasn't afraid to ride a calf—just scared of his mother's reaction if he got himself injured. "I can't get hurt. I just can't." We headed to the corral.

"You ain't gonna get hurt. Don't worry about it," I said. I shooed Jack Knife, my pet calf, into the chute. She was rank. She'd dumped me off probably fifty times.

"I won't flank her, Chuck. Then she won't be too bad."

"Okay." Chuck climbed into the chute. He pulled on the huge helmet with its face mask, took the strap up all the way, and it still didn't touch his chin. When he nodded his head, the helmet wobbled around.

"Ready?"

"Yeah, okay."

"No, Chuck. You've got to say 'outside' or something."

"Outside," he yelled.

I swung the gate open and Jack Knife jumped out across the corral. She hit the ground, backed up, and sent Chuck head-over-heels like a wadded-up candy wrapper. He flipped and rolled through piles of dirt and hit the ground sending dust clouds skyward.

I watched Jack Knife trot away. A sudden scream split the air bringing my attention back to Chuck.

"Oh, God. I'm blind!" he hollered.

I hurried over.

"I'mmmm blind! I'm blind," Chuck's cry sounded muffled. He wiggled his arms and legs.

"Be still. Your neck's broke." He lay on his back with his head twisted all the way around.

"I'm blind," he said.

"Man, Chuck, that's the least of your worries," I said. "Your neck's broke." This would be a good time to run away from home, I thought. Someone would find poor Chuck. I'd wait and maybe come back when I was grown.

"I'm blind, Terry, don't move me. Get my dad, go get my dad."

"I'll get your mom."

"No!" Chuck wailed. "*Not* my mother."

I reached down and turned Chuck's helmet around, until I saw his face. The helmet had spun around backward on his head during his ride.

"Oh, thanks, Terry." Chuck sighed. "You fixed me!"

Chapter 4

Back when I was a teenager, in order to participate in a youth or high school rodeo, students had to have a parent or guardian's signature. This always held me back because my parents didn't encourage me to rodeo. In fact, they strongly *dis*couraged it.

I used to stay awake at night wishing I knew where to find a guardian. What the heck was a guardian anyway? That single requirement seemed to always end the dream for me. If I could just figure it out and get me a good one to sign the entry forms, I could go to the youth rodeos. There'd be nothing to stop me then.

At the local western store I saw a flyer advertising a bull riding school. I wanted to attend. I picked up a registration form and carried it home.

"Mother, please hear me out. There's a famous, world champion bull rider named Don Gay who lives in Mesquite, Texas." I talked fast so she didn't have a chance to say a word. "He's holding a bull riding school during the Thanksgiving holidays. I won't miss any school. He's gonna teach young bull riders like me..." I tapped my chest, "how to ride bulls so they never, ever get hurt."

She untied her apron, a look of resignation on her face. I don't think she believed that I'd never get hurt, but she saw the writing on the wall, and signed the form.

In 1977 I went to Don Gay's Bull Riding School in Mesquite, Texas. I learned not only how to ride bulls the right way but about the equipment and how to use it and a whole lot about rodeo.

One of the main tools a bull rider uses is a bull rope. It's fourteen to sixteen feet in total length. At its center is a leather handhold attached to a larger piece of braided poly rope. This rope is strapped around the bull's girth and positioned behind his front legs so the handhold is in place on his back. In a sophisticated knot tying technique, the rope is looped and tied so when it's pulled on by someone other than the rider, the handhold can be tightened or loosened for the rider.

A woman from an animal rights group confronted Don Gay one day at a rodeo where he provided livestock. "*You* are mistreating those animals!"

"No, ma'am. We take care of our animals." Donnie said.

She didn't agree. "Those poor bulls buck because they're enraged about the strap wrapped around their testicles."

"*No, ma'am!* Tell you what. You go home, take a rope, and wrap it around your husband's testicles. See if he bucks and kicks or sits real still 'til you let him go."

The flank strap goes around the bull's flank—the area between its back rib and hip. It's similar to the belt a weight lifter wears. It provides support for the bull to push against during the athletic activity of bucking and spinning.

I don't know if she followed Donnie's advice, but he sure gave her something to think about.

Contrary to what some may think, the flank strap's *not* wrapped around a bull's testicles to get him to buck. No one can make a bull buck. A bull bucks because he wants to—it's what he does—not because someone makes him.

I learned quickly at Don Gay's school. I did well and rode a lot of bulls. In fact, at the three day school none of them bucked me off.

They'd load a bunch of stock in the bucking chutes. The students, probably thirty of us in all, would choose one to throw our rope around. None of us knew one bull from the other. We all, me included, just climbed on and rode whichever one we happened to pick.

The last day at the school, Don started picking out bulls for me. He'd say, "Throw your rope on that one." Don noticed I'd been staying on and having some success. I'd be about to climb on one and he'd say, "Hey, wait a minute. Hey, you. Get on this bull right here." He never called me by name.

I rode every bull I climbed on during that school. I came home feeling pretty confident and thinking I had to ride *something.*

My brother, Steve, always a big supporter of my rodeo career, helped me a lot. The rodeo arena we started building wasn't completed. We had a corral there but didn't have any rodeo or bucking bulls. I had a solid-red, show calf I named Fire—a Limousine bull. I'd won Grand Champion with him at the Panola County Livestock 4-H Show. He was no slouch but a real good bull. My dad had AI'd [artificially inseminated] some cows to get him. Back then, there wasn't much of that going on in our part of the country. We were downright proud of him.

"That Don Gay Bull Riding School has done turned me into a bull riding mo-chine. I can ride!" I told Steve. "They never bucked me off." I bragged a little and had to get on a bull to show Steve how good I could ride.

"Did Don Gay see it?" Steve asked, eyes wide.

"Yeah, he saw it—saw every one I rode."

"They never bucked you off?" he asked.

"Nope. I never bucked off." I walked over to the chute. "I'm fixin' to ride me a bull."

We had a side delivery gate on our chute where we worked and treated cattle that opened up just like at a rodeo arena. Steve would open the gate for me. I put a flank around Fire. Steve didn't know how to flank one, and I hadn't done it a lot, just a few times at the school.

Fire was just a show bull—fat and gentle. Furry and friendly. He might have been two and a half years old and weighed fourteen hundred pounds. I put him inside that chute and got the rope on him with a bell hanging underneath him. He didn't know what to think. I could tell he was scared.

Steve pulled my bull rope tight for me and went to open the gate.

"He won't buck like the ones at Mesquite," I warned Steve. "Those were professional bulls and a lot of them were featured at the Mesquite Rodeo. He'll buck a little and hop around here. I can at least show you the form they taught me—how to hold my free hand and position my body."

"I understand. I don't expect much from him either." Steve shrugged.

At the school I'd learned you don't say anything when you're ready so as not to give the bull any warning. You just nod your head. I climbed on Fire, scooted up to the rope, and nodded my head. Steve swung that gate open.

Fire kicked straight up and down over his head and turned back spinning right in the gate. He threw me off in a second and a half or less. He performed better than the best bull I'd ridden at the school.

Steve looked at me. "What happened? When are you gonna show me all this fancy bull ridin' stuff you learned at Mesquite?"

I jumped to my feet and dusted off my jeans. "I can't believe that happened. We're runnin' him back in the chute." I shook my head. "Steve, I can ride better than that!"

We ran him through again. That time I got my "hammer cocked," and I kind of understood what to expect. I *knew* how to ride. He did it again, just like the first time. This time, I rode him. He bucked and spun—it was really cool. I couldn't believe my show bull could do so well.

"Hey, man, you *can* ride!" Steve grinned.

"Yeah, I told you I could."

"That was one spinnin' bull."

"Boy, do I know it." I patted Steve on the back.

Fire just stopped as soon as I got off. I walked over and removed my rope and flank strap. I didn't know then that you're supposed to take it easy on a bull that really bucked, but I bet I rode Fire three to four times a week, every week. Every once in awhile he'd toss me off. I'd ride him, and he'd give me his best—bucking and twisting and turning. I practiced on Fire for four or five years and give him a lot of credit for helping me with my career. Fire was all I had. I didn't have several bulls to ride and practice on like some riders.

We started putting on Monday night jackpot bull rides. Guys came out and paid their seven dollar entry fee so they could get on a bull. Fire, number 9, was always the favorite. He didn't have horns, which is what we call a "muley." I'd put him in twice a night. Everybody loved to draw him. Fire was rideable—*if* you knew how to ride. Those who drew him and could ride often won first and second place.

We included him in these jackpot rides for a long time. Fire was still one of our herd bulls and bred our cows. Then he started slowing down. Sometimes he'd just quit bucking. Toward the end of Fire's "rodeo" career, instead of using him for the jackpot rides I'd let someone who didn't know how to ride get on him. He'd make a couple of jumps and a lot of times he'd stop. If the person couldn't ride, Fire never seemed to get to the "stopping" part.

One of the last times I bucked him, a really big, heavy, humongous guy came out to the arena and wanted to get on a bull. It had rained that afternoon, but the ground was in pretty good shape. This very large man climbed up on Fire. Fire jumped out of the chute.

"He's not gonna buck. He'll just hop around a little bit," I told the folks nearby. But Fire had one of his old days again. He turned back and slung this guy through the air. The man landed on his rear end so hard that his britches absolutely exploded. Right where he hit, you could see the "W" of Wrangler imprinted on his backside. Fire stopped in his tracks, turned around, and looked at this guy lying out there with his pants busted wide open.

Well, that's enough, I thought. *He's earned his retirement. This is the last time ol' Fire's gonna buck.* And it was.

Handsome couple, my dad and mom. That's my grandmother's house in the background. From that little white house, she engaged in spy activities—reporting to my mother what I was doing at the corral.

This is my first experience with a "mechanical bull."

My brother, Tim and I are holding one of brother, Steve's 4-H bull calves. Guess what I'm thinking about doing!

Terry, Steve, and Tim, 1965.

This heifer was smelling of Tim. Later this same day, I was denied permission to try to ride her.

I'm doctoring a hurt calf while Tim feeds him a bottle.

I'm trying to teach this heifer how to lead. In the background is the corral where I launched my bull riding career. Steve would put me on weanling calves and run along beside me to hold me on. I got mad and told him, "Turn me loose. I can ride all by myself." So, I was wrong.

My first show steer, Clyde. I was only six. Notice how much bigger he was than me.

I'm posing with a trophy I won for Grand Champion Bull at our local 4-H Livestock Show. I rode him later that week.

My favorite picture of all time, me and my pony Shorty showing out for the camera. He was a great little cow horse and I discovered if I pushed down on his rump he would buck. A cowboy can never get too much practice.

My brothers and I started ranching at an early age. I'm eight years old in this photo.

This is Chuck. What else can I say?

1969. Me with some of my gang, waiting for Friday at 4:00.

That's me on the right; I should have been a model.

Tim and I bagged a 14-point White Tail deer the first time we ever went hunting. We both shot him.

I'm practicing on my 4-H show bull Fire. He's the first bull I got on after attending Don Gay's riding school. I probably rode Fire 75 times and he bucked hard every time.

Chapter 5

A carpet-covered barrel suspended in the middle of four trees, with a garage door spring on each corner, served as my "practice bull" when I was a junior in high school. We had to hang it about ten feet in the air because if we didn't the springs would uncoil and the barrel would hit the ground. To climb on, we had to either pull the barrel down or fetch a ladder. It was wicked and bucked rank but wouldn't spin. It swooped, swayed, and moved in ways a bull wouldn't. We had a lot of fun on it, learned to ride a little and how to dismount, but I knew I'd started to develop some bad techniques.

My brother Tim and I always ran tractors at the ranch. We either cut, raked, or baled hay and mowed pastures pretty much all summer. I always had great thoughts and ideas while I drove a tractor. Still do! One day while driving along cutting hay, an idea for how to build a spinning, bucking barrel that could be mounted on a pedestal came to me. It nearly drove me crazy because I needed to finish the hayfield, but I felt if I didn't stop and write down this idea I'd forget how to build it. I couldn't stand it anymore so I pulled up to the pickup we always left out in the field with us in case something broke down. I parked the tractor, climbed down, and dug through the back of that old truck looking for something to write on. But this idea grew so vivid I actually needed to build it right there.

I found an empty 7-Up can in the back of the pickup. Looking at it, moving it around, I thought... *Yep, that's it.* Using my knife, I split the seam down the length of the can to open it up. I found a wooden Popsicle stick and shoved it inside the opening to serve as a leg. Then to hold it up in place, I took a rusty nail, punched a hole in the can, ran it through the Popsicle stick then through the other side of the can. I could rotate the can and make it move in a bucking motion. I punched another hole in the bottom of the stick and ran rubber bands from there to the end of the can.

My friend Lonnie, already out of high school, worked as a welder. He also rode bulls a little. I decided he'd be the perfect person to help me build it. I showed him what I wanted to do and we put our heads together. We built my idea pretty much like the model I made in the field.

Instead of a can with rubber bands we used a metal barrel and springs from some farm equipment. A piece of pipe cemented in the ground with a bigger diameter section for the leg replaced the Popsicle stick. The pipe slid down over the top of the piece in the ground allowing the barrel to spin. We put a handle on the back of the barrel so it could be bucked from behind and to prevent the rider from seeing or anticipating which direction the "bull" would go next. To finish it off, we covered the exterior with Astroturf.

Our prototype stayed at Lonnie's house a long time and we practiced on it. We wrapped a rope around the barrel several times and tied the end to a tractor or the back of a pickup. Then someone would take off in the truck, pulling the rope and spin the barrel like a toy. It spun so fast you couldn't see which end was which. If you fell off standing up and that handle came around... our technique was kind of dangerous. When we got bucked off we had to hit the ground and stay low.

I decided our creation needed some cushion on it. I got a piece of Naugahyde and padding from an upholstery shop and secured it to the barrel. My dad and brother, Steve, built an arena for me to practice in, and we moved the bucking barrel from Lonnie's house to the arena. After rodeoing professionally and having a little success, I started hosting bull riding schools and used my bucking barrel to teach cowboys how to ride.

Folks would see my training barrel and want one. I loaned mine out several times to different people so they could build their own, but didn't do anything more with the idea until 1993 after Debbie Jo and I'd been married about five years. The price for calves had dropped dramatically. The market was terrible. We needed something to produce income to be able to keep our cattle business going. One day as I glanced at my bucking barrel, the Lord reminded me that he'd given me an idea a long while ago.

What do I call it? The business needed a catchy little name.

The idea came as certainly as God had answered my question. When cowboys ask how good a bull is the reply might be, "he's mighty bucky." That means he'll really buck. So I named it Mighty Bucky.

Along with the name, the Lord also gave me thoughts for changing up the design a little so we could manufacture and market them better. Within a year, we took my 17-year-old idea and created an income-producing business. Deb and I attend trade shows, rodeos, and bull riding schools to promote and sell our line of products. Yeah, there's more than one version to choose from. And we now have a web site, www.mightybucky.com.

Who but the Lord could take something as simple as a pop can with a wooden stick to help create a business for a desperate cowboy and his wife? Seven-Up and Popsicles still make me smile. I wish I had that little 7-Up can with the stick through it!

In bull riding, as in many other professional sports, competitors have to earn membership. A golfer has to qualify in order to compete on the PGA tour. In bull riding, winning a thousand dollars in PRCA sponsored competition allows a competitor to apply for membership. While earning the required amount toward membership, a competitor participates under a permit.

After I reached the thousand dollar winnings goal with my permit, I applied for membership and bought my card. The first year with a card is considered the rookie year and an "F" appears on it, which not only means the cowboy is a rookie but also that he must pay cash for all entry fees. A second year PRCA card has a "C" on it and allows the cardholder to pay entry fees by check.

In January 1978, my senior year in high school, the PRCA started a new program called Permit Sessions. Rodeos have limits on the number of entries and there were so many cardholding bull riders at that time, permit holders couldn't enter and compete. PRCA cardholders had preference. Permit holders occupied the bottom rung, and the opportunities they needed to earn membership just weren't available. To find a rodeo they could enter, permit-holders might have to drive from Texas to Pennsylvania or Michigan.

Implementation of this experimental program took place in Comanche, Texas, on Sunday afternoons at two o'clock. They began the first Sunday of January. Forty to fifty bull riders consistently showed up to try and fill their permits so they could gain PRCA membership and begin their rookie season. Me included. Every Sunday morning I drove over three hundred and fifty miles to Comanche to compete in those sessions where only permit holders competed against each other.

One Sunday I drew a big, fat bull appropriately named Tubby. He took off running down the arena and didn't buck at all. I hadn't drawn any good bulls or won anything at Comanche. The judges decided to give me a re-ride because Tubby didn't buck. This didn't happen very often. Most of the time, if you didn't draw a good bull it was just tough luck.

A little black muley bull stood in the bucking chute. Someone had drawn him but couldn't get out of the gate on him. He could buck and spin so fast he'd generate electricity. If someone sat on him, he bucked inside the chute. He laid down, then stood up, banged the side of the chute, trying to flip himself over. He seemed so mean, he hated himself. The bull threw dirt everywhere and slobbered.

Randy Majors, one of the judges and a well-known bull rider himself, walked over to me. "You're getting a re-ride." He pointed to the little muley. "Can you get out on a chute-fightin' bull?"

Chapter 6

I nodded. "Yeah, I can get out on him." He didn't know I bought bad bulls from the sale barn, took them home, got on them by myself, and even opened the gate with nobody there to help me.

"Then this is your re-ride." Randy wiped sweat off his face with his sleeve.

I eased up over the rails and stood over the bull with my feet on the sides of the chute. Doug pulled my rope tight. Without touching him, I took my wrap and got in position. The black muley trembled and panted. I nodded my head.

Randy stared at me. "Are you sure you're ready?"

I nodded, again.

As the gate cracked open, I sat down. The bull went one jump out of the chute and started spinning fast to the right. He spun so fast he tore a hole in the wind! I rode him, bailed off, and won the bull riding that day.

In the process, I also won the respect of Randy Majors. You have to earn the old-timers' respect. You don't just get it for free. Later on he remembered my willingness to climb on a fussy bull. The reason old-timers respect this ability is because at a rodeo it's not unusual to have a bull like the little muley you can win on. Lots of guys want everything just perfect and exactly right before they nod their heads. To help the rodeo and the stock contractor put on a good show, and to be able to get out of the chute on a bad bull is a skill a true cowboy needs to have.

During those 1978 Permit Sessions I won 894 points— which counted as dollars toward my one-thousand-dollar requirement to apply for PRCA membership and cardholder status. After the sessions finished I kept entering rodeos to hopefully win enough to meet the requirement. I rode well but didn't win anything until July.

That summer I entered the PRCA rodeo in Mesquite, Texas, every Friday night. It was only a two and a half hour drive from home. Often I went up there with Nicky Wheeler, a great bull rider who had gone to the National Finals.

Nicky hosted a riding event in an amateur rodeo on Saturday nights in Tyler, Texas. He still wanted to ride bulls but just didn't want to do it all the time. He'd begun to slow down and didn't want to rodeo as hard as he had been. Nicky had some really good stock and I knew if I wanted to ride professionally, I needed exposure to his top caliber bulls. Nicky's were equal to and sometimes better than those I drew at professional rodeos.

Throughout the summer my schedule stayed the same— Fridays I rode in Mesquite, Saturday nights I competed in Nicky's open rodeo. First place at Nicky's might make a hundred and fifty or sixty dollars. I won a lot. My winnings didn't count toward my PRCA total—the rodeo wasn't sanctioned. It was just money for my pocket.

Finally, I filled my permit the last of July 1978 at Mesquite when I rode Hurricane, a big black bald-faced bull. He didn't just buck but turned back *and* bucked. I made a great ride.

So did Nicky. He rode a big yellow muley that turned back. Anybody who'd ever ridden him knew this bull looked good and rode easy. Named Easy Money, that's exactly what he was, because if you rode him, you won something. Nicky scored more on his ride than I did.

A bull ride is judged on a hundred point scale. There are two judges, each with fifty points to disperse. One to twenty-five points for the rider and one to twenty-five for the bull. The bull and rider scores are added together for the total. Even if a rider gets thrown and doesn't make the eight second buzzer or receive a score, the bull does. This score is used for future rodeo competitions.

A cowboy named Glenn Sullivan rode a bull called G-2 Time Out. Glenn rode bulls real pretty. Time Out jumped and kicked around the arena in a circle.

I was the new kid on the block. I thought my score would win, but Glenn scored more than I did, too. I came in third, won about three hundred dollars, but most important, I made enough to earn my PRCA membership.

The season ended in the fall. I could have continued competing with my permit for a few months afterward and that's what I should have done. My rookie year would have been the 1979 season. I won over $20,000 that year and just missed National Finals. I would have won Rookie of the Year if I hadn't gone ahead and bought my membership so soon. At the time, I didn't know how it worked and wish someone had told me. I would have waited! In the big picture of things it's not so important, but it would have been nice.

I'd seen Glenn at Nicky's in Tyler and he rode every once in a while. So, I knew who he was and knew he rode well. Glenn came up to me afterward. "You should have won the bull riding tonight. I'm sorry the judges thought Nicky and I rode better. Honestly, you made the best ride."

Nicky told me the same thing later. My goal had always been just to be able to hold my own against those great bull riders. I wanted to be a competitive threat to the top riders. I found out that night I was, and knowing it rewarded me better than all the money I could have won.

Glenn came across as real nice, quiet, and shy. Around amateur and open rodeo, he was the big dog—two or three years older than me. I got to know him better when he started coming over to Nicky's on Saturday nights more often. Back then there weren't a lot of Christians around rodeo, at least not many who'd admit to being one. Glenn watched me and saw how I lived. "Are you a Christian?" he asked one day.

"You bet I am."

"I haven't been one for very long, but I'm one, too," he said. With our faith in common, we struck up a friendship.

"What're your plans?" I asked Glenn after one of the Saturday night rodeos.

"What do you mean? What are *your* plans?" he shot back with a grin.

"I'm gonna make a living ridin' bulls. I'm in training and learning to win at this level. I ain't stayin' around here. I'm plannin' to shoot for the National Finals and ride bulls where they give away lots of money."

"Well, that's what I'm after," Glenn said.

I brushed the dust off my cowboy hat and stuck it back on my head. "I've been lookin' for a guy to travel with who doesn't drink and chase women. I don't want to mess with all that. I'll go by myself before I'll go with someone who parties."

"Well, it ain't no secret," he shook his head. "I might would've been one of those guys before, but I'm not now. I want the same thing you do."

We formed a partnership and decided to pursue this dream of qualifying for the NFR, together. I'd been thinking about what I needed in a partner. I wanted somebody with me who rode well—better than me, in fact—and would push me to ride better. I needed someone confident. The worst thing that could happen would be to have a partner who wasn't riding well and as a result, became depressed. Their discouragement would wear off on me and drag me down.

Glenn and I started traveling together the 1979 season, which actually started in November of 1978 with a big rodeo in Kansas City, Missouri. That rodeo gave everybody hope— the first chance to get off to a good start.

Right before Kansas City, Jonesville, Louisiana held a little PRCA rodeo. I made the phone call to enter Glenn and me in the event. "This is Terry Holland. I want to enter the bull riding at Jonesville, Louisiana."

"Are you buddying?" the operator asked.

"Yes, with Glenn Sullivan." The buddy system guaranteed we would compete together the same night instead of one of us riding Thursday and the other on Saturday.

Confidence is one thing you've got to have in any sport. Glenn and I felt we could ride as well as anybody, but it was important to *know* for sure before we jumped in to compete against seasoned cowboys at the big rodeos.

Filled with self-assurance, we arrived in Jonesville and asked about our bulls. We competed in our event and stayed on for the required eight seconds. Glenn and I both placed.

We knew Jonesville was a small town, small rodeo, and we wouldn't be seeing a whole lot more of those in our *big* plans. For us, bigger, better rodeos lay ahead—Odessa, Denver, San Antonio, and Fort Worth—where we'd be competing against the very best. In those days the great riders won at those rodeos. Tough competition and good money. The very best bull riders in the world rode in the PRCA because if they wanted to compete big time in a lot of rodeos, they didn't have other options. There wasn't a PBR (Professional Bull Riders) tour anywhere. Now, it's split up with great bull riders in both the PBR and the PRCA.

Glenn and I got our feet wet together. We laughed, had lots of fun, and enjoyed friends, but we didn't do anything to compromise our career goals or our Christian walk. We were strictly business and there to ride.

I had a 1978 Buick Skylark for transportation when Glenn and I partnered up. We drove home toward Carthage one night after we'd ridden three nights in a row at Bay City, Texas; Jacksonville, Florida; and San Angelo, Texas. We'd planned to go from Bay City to San Angelo and *then* to Jacksonville, but that's not how it worked out.

After all those miles and competing in three different rodeos, we were dog-tired and wanted to get home. By three in the morning, I was bringing it on, going about seventy miles an hour. At Mt. Enterprise, eighteen miles from the house, we hit a deer head-on. The impact knocked the hood loose. It folded up over the car blocking the windshield. I rolled the window down, stuck my head out, and managed to get my car to the side of the road.

I called my daddy, like I'd done a bunch of times. He came and rescued us, but problems on the road never stopped me. I loved driving long hours to and from the rodeos. Glenn never did, but as long as we split the bills, it worked just fine.

In the spring of 1979, Glenn and I drove to a rodeo in Dothan, Alabama. The bull I climbed on had real long horns that stuck straight up. He jumped out of the chute, kicked, and stumbled in the dirt. He went down to his knees. The momentum slung me out over his horns, and when he raised his head, he hit me just under my right eye. I sprung a leak and bled all over the place.

Neither of us won any money that time.

Everyone who saw my injury worried over it. Glenn frowned at the gash. "Terry, that wound needs stitchin'."

But it was Saturday night.

"Aw, we ain't goin' to the hospital—that's too much of a hassle. My uncle will sew it up for free when we get home." Back home, my Uncle Virgil was our family's doctor.

A paramedic checked my injury. "It'll probably take about fourteen stitches. It's going to swell and the longer you wait, the harder it'll be to clean it up and prevent it from scarring."

I shrugged. "It won't hurt to let it go."

The paramedic handed me a small bag filled with ice. "If you'll keep ice on it, the swelling won't be as bad."

"Let's just get it fixed here," Glenn said. I could tell he thought I was crazy for not getting it stitched up at the local hospital.

"Nah, I can make it. Let's go home." We tossed our rigging bags into the trunk of my Buick.

Dothan, Alabama, meant about fourteen hours to get home. We were both tired already. And the paramedic was right about the swelling. I wasn't in any shape to drive. "You're gonna have to drive, Glenn."

Glenn nodded. "I can do it."

We went north from Alabama to Jackson, Mississippi, and headed west on Interstate 20. The hour before dawn is the hardest time to drive. I saw Glenn shake his head and rub his eyes, trying to stay awake. I couldn't hold on any longer. Finally, I dozed off.

I woke to screeching tires—roooooaaarh—as we skidded sideways.

Chapter 7

We spun 180 degrees and came to a stop in the lane. Glenn's eyes were big. He nearly stood on the brake pedal. Sweat formed across his forehead.

The force shoved my injured face to within inches of the windshield. Ready to scream on impact, I grabbed the dash in a death grip and rocked back into the seat as the car stopped, a safer distance from the windshield.

I looked over at my partner. "Glenn! What happened? What are you doin'?"

"Did you see that mule?" he asked.

"What? I was asleep!"

"Y-you didn't see a white mule run across the road?"

I looked in the ditch and all around the area. "A white mule?"

"Uh, just forget it," Glenn said. We took off and headed down the interstate. The incident had us both wide awake now.

"What do you mean a white mule?" I questioned him.

"Ah, nothin'. Just forget it." He turned his attention to driving.

I didn't let him forget it. To this day, I still ask him, "You seen a white mule lately?"

By the time we made it safely to my folks' house where I lived, my wound had swelled and split open. Uncle Virgil met me at the clinic and sewed me up. The injury healed and there's barely a scar. Dr. V. M. Holland took care of me many times and kept me going. I gave him plenty of practice stitching skin back together.

I called and entered Glenn and me in the rodeo at Kansas City. Excited but nervous, this was our first shot at the "big time" and the first opportunity to ride in a rodeo that size. We called to find out which day we were scheduled to compete. Two days later, we made a call to learn which bulls we'd drawn. I drew a bull named Y-93. Glenn drew one called R.L.

I'd never been on an airplane before—never even seen one up close. We made reservations and Glenn and I flew to Missouri. We tried to rent a car, but neither of us had a credit card. After much discussion, pleading, and a cash deposit, we were able to get a rental and drove to the rodeo grounds.

The number one bull riding stock contractor in the world at the time—and the company providing livestock for this rodeo—was the Steiner Rodeo Company out of Austin, Texas. They'd been in the rodeo business for years and had great, awesome, legendary bulls.

Glenn's bull had a reputation for being mean as the devil but one you'd want to draw because you could win the rodeo, *if* you rode him. Nearly impossible to get away from, he'd already hooked about ten cowboys in a row. Glenn climbed on R.L., took a wrap, scooted up to his rope, and nodded. R.L. blasted through the gate like his tail was on fire. Glenn stayed on and rode him. The whistle blew. Glenn jumped off and hit the ground, but didn't make it to the fence.

R.L. mowed him down, circled, and ran back toward him. Glenn managed to get to his hands and knees. Just as he looked up, one of R.L.'s horns caught Glenn right in the head. It didn't knock him out but raised a little knot in the middle of his forehead.

Y-93. He was a bad cat, one of the most dreaded bulls in professional rodeo at the time, but I didn't know it. Even if I had, it wouldn't have mattered. I thought I could ride any bull.

"Which one's Y-93?" I asked some of the more experienced bull riders. "Show him to me."

One of the cowboys pointed. "You see that pen where all the bulls look like they're lying down and there's one standing up? That's him, right there. And, well, they're *all* standing up."

A great big red bull, Y-93 had huge horns and a white star on his forehead.

"What does he do?" I asked.

"He turns back to the right after about three jumps, spins to the right, and bucks away from you. And he's real welly," the cowboy said.

"Welly?" I asked, trying not to seem ignorant.

"That means the inside of the spin. If a bull is spinning to the right, he wants you down on the inside of that spin where he can work on you with those horns," he explained. "Y-93 is real welly."

Stay out of the well, I repeated in my head. *Whatever you do, Terry, don't go down in that well.* I thought about it for about an hour and a half. Meditated on it.

I got on him. Sure enough—three jumps and he started spinning to the right. Immediately, I fell into the well. I guess I'd thought about it too much. Y-93 whacked me right up side the head with his horn and knocked me unconscious.

I hit the ground, and honestly, the only memory I have of that trip is the lady giving us a hard time when we rented our car. I can relate the incident and facts only because I saw them on video later.

One of the old cowboys around the ranch used to tell me, "To keep from gettin' run over by one of those bad bulls, be perfectly still and they won't hurt you." I found out with Y-93 how wrong he was.

It's amazing how perfectly still you can lie when you're knocked unconscious. I wasn't twitching a muscle, yet Y-93 spun around, spotted me, and gathered me up with those big horns of his before the bull fighters could get there. He threw me across Kemper arena. I tumbled around and came to my senses midair. Landing on my feet, I ran away from the bull to Bobby Steiner, the rodeo stock contractor. He caught me in his arms and I fell. I didn't know where I was, how I'd gotten there, or how to get home. For several minutes, I didn't even recognize Glenn. I was downright scared. I ended up spending a bunch of money at the hospital for x-rays.

The Kansas City rodeo had what's called a short round. After a whole week of rodeo events, the last performance— the finals—only included the top twelve scoring cowboys. Glenn made the short round. He and I had joked about how cool it would be to win at Kansas City and I envisioned myself winning. Instead, I went home depressed and discouraged with myself but happy for Glenn's success. He flew home with me to make sure I made it okay, then he went back to compete in the finals.

Before we reached home, the story had already made the news. "East Texas cowboy trampled, nearly gored to death."

"Was that you?" my mother asked when I came in. She knew it was.

"He just knocked me out. He didn't trample or gore me, or anything close to that. He just scooped me up and tossed me." *About forty feet through the air.*

I felt dejected, embarrassed. Maybe my mother was right when she'd said, "You're gonna get killed out there." I'd come close to it. Maybe this wasn't for me after all.

Glenn called from Kansas City and told me he'd drawn a bull named V-1. A tough one to ride, this bull had earned the designation, "eliminator." If a cowboy had good judges and could ride, he could possibly win something on him. V-1 didn't have nice form or look pretty; he was just downright ugly to ride. Glenn rode V-1 and won, which put him number one in the world—in the top spot right off the bat.

After getting smacked in the head, knocked out, and having my dream of winning evaporate, I had to make a decision—do I go forward and live my dream or listen to what everyone else thought was common sense?

I'd worked so hard! I couldn't give up. Instead, I persevered.

Denver was our next big rodeo. It ran for nearly two weeks, and we stayed for the duration. Glenn drew the best there, C-13 Top Cat, a famous rank bull. I also drew an excellent bull and scored 78. Friends from back home saw the scores from the major rodeos in the Dallas newspaper. Up until the last performance I was winning.

Don Gay rode a good bull and scored 85. He won that first go-round.

I placed second.

Glenn made a fantastic ride on Top Cat, but his hand popped out of the rope right at the whistle. I don't think anyone would have complained if the judges had gone ahead and given him a score, but they didn't. He might have beaten Donnie and won several thousand dollars to add to his prize money. If he'd won, it would have changed his whole season.

Glenn and I made trips to Kansas City, Denver, and Fort Worth to compete. Glenn did well in Kansas City and I won $1,500 in Denver.

Chapter 8

Two duds. That's what I drew for the Fort Worth rodeo's 1979 season. Glenn started off better than I did. He drew two good bulls, Evil Weevil and Black Bart, but didn't ride either of them. Neither of us won a thing.

We drove to San Antonio to compete in a rodeo held at the Jim Freeman Coliseum. It ran for at least twelve performances. For the weekend shows, with only three performances left, the top thirty-six riders came back and competed in a progressive short round or finals. Twelve cowboys rode Saturday night, twelve more contended Sunday at the matinee, and the last twelve rode Sunday night.

The bull I drew for Saturday afternoon bucked a little bit and the judges gave me a mediocre score of 67—my lowest all winter. By now the schedule we'd been keeping had worn us out. I didn't think a 67 would put me into the finals and figured if I can't win it, I might as well go home. So I started putting my gear away.

"Hey, wait," one of the cowboys said. "Better check and see. You might have made the finals."

I frowned. "With a sixty-seven?"

"Yeah. They're taking thirty-six guys. Go look before you leave." He pointed toward the rodeo office.

Embarrassed with my low score, I didn't even want to ask the secretary if I'd made it. But I asked anyway.

"Let me check." She started at the top.

"I won't be up there. Look low on the list."

She ran her finger to the bottom. "Yep. Terry Holland, number thirty-six. You'll be in the short round and ride tonight."

I shrugged. "Do you know which bull I have?"

"Jiggs Butler's bull number two," she said. "No name, just a number."

"You've got to be kiddin' me!" Suddenly, I didn't feel so tired anymore. Jiggs' Two had to be one of the best bulls to draw in rodeo at that time. A big black bull without horns, Jiggs' Two would buck. He tossed off lots of guys, but if someone could ride him, he could win. I needed to make up a lot of ground, because the overall score would count toward my total.

I left the office and found Glenn to tell him my news.

To this day, it's probably one of the very best rides I ever made. Jiggs' Two turned back in the gate as soon as it opened. Kicking straight over his head, he spun with the grace of a dancer and drifted his way down the arena. He bucked into my hand, making the ride an advantage for me! Eight seconds ticked past in slow motion. As the ride unfolded, I couldn't believe the perfection of how it felt. It seemed to be one of those magical, amazing, wonderful times. Above the sounds of the bull and my concentration on riding well, I heard the audience in the packed arena scream and holler. Jiggs' Two continued his powerful performance into the middle of the arena.

The whistle blew and I jumped off. A lot of the great, top bull riders of that era saw me ride a fantastic bull, and it gave them a taste of what I could do.

"It's an eighty, ladies and gentlemen," said the announcer. "What a ride."

I couldn't believe it. Earlier in the same rodeo, one of the greatest bull rides I'd ever seen scored a 78. Back then, an 80 was a high score, and it threw me into the lead for that short go-round. I held the highest average score, so far, for two rides. I started with a dud, added an 80, and suddenly I became the guy to beat. Then it hit me. If things held out, I'd win several thousand dollars. I called my dad from one of those old wooden pay phone booths in the coliseum. "Man, Daddy, I just scored eighty points at San Antonio."

"I thought you scored sixty-seven," he said.

Disappointed with my earlier low score, I hadn't even called to let him know I'd made the short round. "Yeah, for my first ride. You won't believe it. I made a great ride on Jigg's Two and scored eighty points!"

"Is it over? How much you gonna win?" he asked.

"Two performances left. I don't know for sure, but I might win pretty big." Glenn walked with me to check and see which bulls the other good riders had drawn for the next two performances. I wanted to check the competition to see who could potentially beat me. The winners wouldn't be declared until after everyone finished riding Sunday evening.

Randy Majors drew a bull named Mean Joe Green. Randy had been one of the judges at the permit session in Comanche, Texas, about a year ago and had given me the re-ride. I turned to Glenn. "Oh, man. He'll beat me. I've seen that bull before and he's unbelievable."

"Your bull was unbelievable, too," he said. "You'll win the short round."

"You think so?"

Glenn nodded. "I've seen Mean Joe Green, but you made an outstanding ride."

I left San Antonio Saturday evening after I rode in the final round and drove to another rodeo. Sunday evening I waited and waited. I couldn't stand it and called the rodeo secretary at San Antonio late that night from somewhere on the road. "Is the rodeo over?"

"Not quite, Terry. Call back in about thirty minutes."

The suspense nearly killed me. I called again later. "Did Randy Majors ride that bull?"

"Yep. He rode him."

I sighed. "Well, second ain't bad."

"Oh, no. Not second. He scored seventy-nine," she said.

I knew someone else had scored more than I did for the overall total. I sure wanted to win that short round. Ended up, I won the short round and took third overall. I added the $4,000 prize to my other winnings and brought my total to $6,000.

I flew from Dallas to Tucson for the next competition. Of all people who could be on the same plane, here came Randy Majors. "Well, I guess you're that guy who cost me winning short round at San Antone," he said.

"Yeah, I guess so." I slung my bag over my shoulder.

"You drew a nice bull, but you won't draw nice bulls like that the whole year. I guarantee you." He smiled, continuing to pick on me a little. "You're going to be grease in the frying pan. Fry up pretty quick, and there won't be nothin' left of you."

"You never know. I might hang around longer than you think." I certainly hoped so.

"What did you draw for Tucson?" he asked.

"Four M."

He nodded. We both knew Four M. Another black muley, he spun real fast like Jiggs' Two. Randy got bucked off at Tucson. I won second. He kidded me that whole season, because I'd beaten him and managed to stay ahead of him in the standings.

Even though Glenn rode his second bull at Denver, the disappointment over not getting a score after riding Top Cat took a foothold and began to work on him. Glenn got cold. He stopped winning. Several more situations happened that season like the one at Denver and he became discouraged. By July—the time to rodeo hard—Glenn ran out of money and had to go home and work. We stayed in touch, remained friends, went to an occasional rodeo together, but I had to find another partner.

One of the most famous bulls I rode during my career cost me over $20,000. Number GM-12, a short, stocky, Charolais-cross without horns; Joe Cool. He belonged to Neal Gay from Mesquite, Texas. Neal not only hosted the Mesquite Rodeo, he also provided stock for other rodeos. He owned a lot of great bulls, but Joe Cool had to be one of the very best.

Joe Cool came from the Nacogdoches, Texas area. Even though he was cream-colored with curly hair on his face, folks called him Ol' Yella Dog when he first started out. His gentleness made him unique. He was just a big, friendly pet. He turned into one of the greatest bulls in bull riding history. I'd seen him at a lot of rodeos. I'd seen him on television. He became so famous he even had a fan club in New York City and his fans wore "Joe Cool" tee shirts.

Everywhere Joe Cool bucked, the rodeos started and ended with bull riding. He provided atmosphere. He started the rodeo and bucked first. Always. People came to the rodeo just for the chance Joe Cool would throw some dirt on them. They'd try to catch it and, if successful, put it in a little bottle. Even nontraditional rodeo fans and tourists often came to see Joe Cool.

I woke up at night dreaming about climbing on Joe Cool's broad back. I wanted to ride him. If I could just get on him—he spins to the right and I'm right-handed... if only!

While still in high school and just a permit holder, I drew Joe Cool for one of the Friday night rodeos at Mesquite. And after I drew him, I wasn't quite so eager. I felt terrified, horrified, mystified. Scarified!

When I showed up at the rodeo that day I'd seen a bunch of young kids sitting on the fence petting Joe Cool, scratching his ears, and trying to get on him. Wherever they scratched, he leaned toward them and up against the fence.

I went closer. "Man, I've seen you, but I never really looked at you like this!" I saw his brand, GM-12, and watched those kids touch him. He can't be *that* bad; I tried to convince myself. *A bull that'll let little children scratch and pet him—why, he wouldn't buck me off.*

I hadn't done a thing at that point; I'd never won money in a pro rodeo. Me, a nobody—just a permit holder and I'd drawn Joe Cool. Even though Joe Cool allowed little kids to pet him, I was afraid.

Today Neal Gay, the stock contractor, is my friend. He calls and checks on me once in awhile, but back then he only knew me as high school boy with big dreams. I remember him asking, "Now, who got Joe Cool?"

From my perch on the back of the chutes I raised my hand. Bulls lined the alleyway getting ready. Joe Cool stood in the chute. Sweat trickled down my back.

Chapter 9

Neal looked me over. "They're gonna be singing that National Anthem. You be on him and be gettin' ready. When they get to the part about the land of the free and the home of the brave, you'd better have your hand in the rope with your wrap made and the rope tied like you want it. 'Cause you're fixin' to be noddin' your head just a few seconds after that."

The last thing I wanted was to have Neal Gay yell at me and use raunchy language to chew me out for not being ready.

Home of the free and land of the brave? When is that part? I was so nervous I couldn't remember the National Anthem, how it went, or anything about it! The singing started and I climbed onto Joe Cool. My buddy, Doug Barkley, stood by to pull my rope—both of us big-eyed and scared.

"Start pulling it right now," I said.

Doug shook his head. "He said not to do it 'til the 'land of the free and home of the brave.'"

"Yeah, but I'm gonna have it done and whenever they get to that part, I know I'll be ready!"

Even though the singer had barely started the National Anthem, I pulled my rope and I'd already taken my wrap.

Neal Gay said (and I'll have to leave out most of what he told me), "What are you doin'? I told you *not* to take your wrap or be ready until the land of the free and the home of the brave. That's at the *end* of the song, son! Not at the first of it."

So I loosened my rope to start over. I'd barely gotten it undone before Neal hollered at me again.

"Hurry up! Take a wrap and get yourself ready."

Finally, I heard those words. The time to ride had arrived. I scooted up.

"And the home... of the... brave," the singer and crowd sang together.

The gate swung open.

Joe Cool bucked me off hard and fast. He went from a gentle pet to a violent explosion. He turned back to the right. I responded like I thought I should and he threw me.

Back in the old days at Mesquite they had chicken wire netting up behind the fence between the arena and stands. The chicken wire made the fence hard to climb. If a bull came after a rider, the wire barrier made getting out of his way tough.

A lot of times bull riders would laugh, joke around, and say, "That bull threw me out of the arena." Joe Cool threw me with so much force, if it hadn't been for the netting, he would have thrown me clear into the stands. I hit the chicken wire and just melted down the fence. I lay there looking up at him.

Joe Cool acted like he didn't want to step on anybody or hurt them. He'd even pick up his foot and seem to try to miss a guy. He bucked with a vengeance, but the moment he threw someone off, he stopped. Then he'd walk over toward the fence and rub his head around in the dirt. Nobody pushed him. They let him take his time.

Lying on the ground, all wadded up in a clump, nursing my wounds, I watched Joe Cool. He wallowed around and threw arena dirt up into the stands as people tried to catch it. Finally, he just meandered out of the arena to a standing ovation.

I climbed on Joe Cool nine times during my career and only rode him twice. One of my best rides on him took place at Mesquite where I won $650. My second ride happened at the Texas Circuit Finals in Ft. Worth. Although this was a real tough event with a lot of excellent bull riders participating, it never paid very much. I rode him there and made $328. Both rides combined gained me less than a thousand dollars.

Joe Cool bucked me off one of those times at a big invitational bull ride at Billy Bob's in Fort Worth where the winner took home $20,000. Guess I choked on the money. He bucked just as good for $328 as he did for $20,000.

Joe Cool had gone to the National Finals six or seven different times and was rarely, if ever, ridden. About 1982, Neal Gay retired this champion bucking bull and put him in

Don's back yard where Joe Cool would come up to the fence or the back of the house. They have pictures of Don and his wife, Terri, hugging on this bull like he was a big, puppy dog. I thought it was a neat way for Joe Cool to spend his last days. One great bull.

A lot of times when I went to Mesquite, there were two kinds of bulls—those like Joe Cool with some experience and others that had never been bucked before. Why, some of them had never even been to town. Neal Gay would buy bulls out of south Louisiana and truck them up to Mesquite. They'd buck them at the rodeo just to find out how good they were and if any of them were worth keeping. Sometimes the bulls were mean; they'd fight and try to hook the cowboys or chase them, but they didn't buck very well. Other bulls at Mesquite were just plain bad.

I remember drawing a bull one time that I knew had never been bucked. I could tell by how violently he fought the chute. With the name Jack the Ripper, I should have suspected I might be in trouble.

Nowadays a bull's horns have to be tipped or cut off so they're blunt. Back then, there weren't a lot of rules and they'd left Jack the Ripper's horns pointed. This was also before bull riders wore safety equipment of any kind to protect us from getting gored.

After watching Jack the Ripper in the alley and chute, I had second thoughts. *Man, this would have been a good one to turn out.* (In other words, I could pay my entry fee, but not get on him.) *Well, you never know. He might buck.*

One of the rodeo clowns walked up to me. "Son, when you get off this bull, you'd better be runnin'."

I'd already decided to do just that. I climbed on him. They opened the gate. Jack the Ripper took off running. He hooked at the wind, gouged at my legs, and reached around with his horns to try and hook me off his back. He made it hard to stay on, but I rode him. The whistle blew—time to get off. I knew I had a terrible score and didn't win anything because he didn't buck at all. Jack the Ripper just ran around the arena. I jumped off and managed to keep my feet under me pretty good.

"Hey, bull! Hey, bull!" the clown yelled and waved his arms. "Run, son, run!"

I didn't know the clown or bull's location, but I took off running as hard and fast as I could. *Don't look back, Terry. Do not look back. If you do, you'll fall or something will happen.*

The audience noise roared. Women screamed. I couldn't stand it. I *had* to look. Over my shoulder to the left. He came right behind me. His pointed horns seemed to stick out three to four feet on each side. He bore down on me. Snot went everywhere—his *and* mine. I ran as fast as I could run, but looking back is *not* what you want to do.

If this bull hooks me it ain't gonna be funny. He'll run that horn through and kill me. I'll bleed all over the place and die right here in this arena.

The bull came closer.

I stumbled but kept going. It seemed everything moved in slow motion like in a dream where something is chasing you and closing in.

When a bull is getting ready to hook someone, he'll bounce stiff-legged on his front feet.

I saw him bounce. I knew he was fixin' to turn his head sideways and run a horn into me. Right before the fence I tripped and started to fall. I scrambled, pushing out my chest and curving my back. I could feel his horn rake my shirt.

I wore my shirt starched and a little big to give me room to ride. It puffed out in the back. Jack the Ripper stabbed at me and hooked my shirt, ripping the back completely out of it. With the momentum he'd gained charging after me, I'm sure he expected to get some of my flesh to shish-kabob. He missed the meat, but as I found later, came close enough to make a red mark across my back. He dove forward on past me, hanging his horn deep into the dirt.

I scrambled up on the railing.

Jack the Ripper flipped over, spun around, and chased me up the fence.

Exact opposites. On one side, you got Joe Cool. On the other side, Jack the Ripper. And me, there in the middle.

Here's one of our herd bulls standing in front of my bucking barrel. That's just plain cool, if you ask me!

I'm practicing on the bucking barrel Lonnie and I first made.

Me with Daddy making a game plan before a high school rodeo in Center, Texas. After he understood my level of commitment, he became one of my biggest fans.

During my senior year in high school, my dad and brother, Steve, built a state-of-the-art rodeo arena for me to practice in. By then, they'd all decided it was too late to talk me out of riding, so they pitched in to help me get good at it.

My first professional traveling partner and good friend, Glenn Sullivan, sticking it on one and looking pretty.

Here I'm practicing in our corral. That's my dad catching the gate and my best friend J. D. Barkley climbing the fence.

Riding at an open rodeo in Marshall, Texas, when I was 17. I'd go to three or four of these rodeos each weekend. Sometimes by the end of the weekend, I'd won around $400. Shoot—that's better than working!

I won my first belt buckle as high school Saddle Bronc Champion.
(4ᵗʰ from left).

My favorite bull of all time, hands down, was Neal Gay's GM12 Joe Cool. This photo was taken at Nacogdoches, Texas, in 1980. I rode him twice in eight attempts and won about $900 combined. He bucked me off for $20,000 at Billy Bob's in Ft. Worth. I guess I choked! Photo by: Huffman Foto.

This picture was snapped right before Y93 knocked me out in Kansas City, 1979. Photo by: Bern Gregory, Black Jack, Missouri

World Champion Don Gay and my dad help out during a practice session at our arena in Carthage.

RL of the Steiner Rodeo Company was probably one of the hardest bulls to get away from after a ride. He hooked everybody. I drew him and rode at the Houston Astrodome (the largest arena in the business) in 1979. Photo by: Huffman Foto.

Winning 2nd place out of 85 bull riders at my first rodeo. I'd told my dad I'd quit riding if I didn't win something. I woke him up when I got home and showed him my check for $102.

Chapter 10

Nineteen years old in 1979, I was just a young fellow getting my rodeo career started. Lots of big rodeos take place during the Fourth of July holiday. I'd bucked off nine or ten bulls in a row at some of the best ones. I'd been having a tough time.

The rodeo in Nampa, Idaho is a big one. I'd already spent almost two thousand dollars more than what I had in the bank. I really needed to win something. You know, usually, it doesn't help at all when you need to win so desperately.

At Nampa I drew the same bull Glenn had drawn at Denver—the really famous rank C-13 Top Cat. I'd drawn and ridden him earlier in the year at Clovis, New Mexico, where I only scored 68 points. Instead of bucking like the legendary great bull I knew him to be, he went way down the arena before turning back.

All the great bull riders had been on Top Cat at one time or another. Some had ridden him; some hadn't.

Roy Carter, a good friend of mine and a talented bull rider, pulled my rope and helped me in the bucking chute that night. He was older than me and someone I looked up to. Roy encouraged me.

"Terry, do you know John Quintana?" Roy asked before my event.

I shook my head. "Well, nah. But I know who he is!"

John was the world champion back in 1972. He'd ridden a bull—a legendary ride, I suppose—in Gladewater, Texas and scored 94 points in 1971. They even put a sign on the bucking chute that said "this is the chute that John Quintana rode V61, 1971 for 94 points." It was one of the greatest rides ever. But I'd never met him or even seen him in person. I knew he'd retired and lived near Nampa, Idaho.

"Terry, this is John Quintana," Roy introduced us.

"Terry Holland." We shook hands. I couldn't believe it! Not only did I get to meet him, but John Quintana stood on the back of the chute with Roy and me while I got ready to ride.

I'll never forget it. Man, just telling it makes me nervous. And boy, was I nervous then. This man was a legend.

"Terry, do you want this bull to turn back and buck with you?" John said.

"You bet I do, John. I rode him at Clovis, New Mexico. He bucked hard, but didn't spin. And I didn't win anything."

"Well, you're gonna win something on him tonight," John said. "I'm gonna turn him back right in the gate and make him spin as soon as it opens."

"How're you goin' to do that?" I asked.

"Do you want him to?" He looked at me from beneath his cowboy hat.

"Yessir." I nodded.

"Then, you just worry about ridin' him. I'll worry about getttin' him to spin." He smiled.

If I can ride him, this will be a great story to tell some day when I'm old.

John stepped down in the arena.

I looked over at Roy. "What's he gonna do?"

"Don't worry about it, Terry. Just bear down and ride him." Roy pulled my rope.

I slid up, nodded my head, and the gate popped opened.

John Quintana took his hat off and just as C13 Top Cat jumped out of the chute, John slapped him and shook his hat right in the bull's face. Turning back, that bull spun right in the gate and bucked!

The whistle blew. I made an eight-second qualified ride and jumped off. The crowd went crazy. I scored 88 points—a huge score in those days. At the time, it was the highest score I'd ever had. I thought I'd experienced one of the greatest rides of my life. And, at 19 years old, just starting out, it was.

"Great ride." John shook my hand.

"Thank you for making him buck," I said.

I won $3,000 at the Nampa rodeo. I'll never forget that awesome, special night. Barbara Mandrell sang at the rodeo the same evening. I remember her singing "If Lovin' You Is Wrong, I Don't Wanna Be Right." What a great time.

I rode C13 Top Cat again the next year at Sidney, Iowa. He bucked somewhere in between, I guess, because I scored 78 on him there. That's one great bull I rode three different times and scored 68, 78, and 88 on him.

More than twenty years later we were at a trade show in Las Vegas at the NFR. One of the vendors sold memorabilia and collectibles. She took old advertising posters from different rodeos and put them on wood frames. I stopped to look through them and noticed something with Nampa on it. I flipped through the rest of the pictures to it. "Nampa, Idaho! July 19th to 21st, 1979! Featuring Barbara Mandrell, Country Music Female Vocalist of the Year," the advertisement read. Barbara's picture smiled from the poster.

I don't recall what the woman charged me for that poster, but I had to have it. It's up on the wall at home.

I drew Y-93 again the following August at a rodeo in Missouri. Down in the well I went, again. He smacked me in the face so hard it didn't hurt, but blood flew everywhere. This time, he broke my nose.

After spending the night at the hospital and deciding I'd never ride Y-93 again, I flew the following day to Kankakee, Illinois. No kidding, I actually rode the next day at a two o'clock matinee and won on a bull called Ravioli. I wore glasses back then. My face swelled so much, my glasses sat somewhere upon my forehead. I couldn't feel my teeth for nearly two weeks.

Sometimes things look bad. You get discouraged with life, and it's really tough. I've learned if you catch hold of the vision, then you *can't* stop. I couldn't stop what had already been put in motion. Three months later, at the tender age of nineteen, I became the number-two-ranked bull rider in the world of professional rodeo.

Back in 1980, before I'd even turned twenty-one, the PRCA decided to finally make some rules to help bull riders. One thing they did was give the judges in the arena a backup stopwatch.

Many times at the rodeo, if a secretary worked for the stock contractor, she might be, let's just say, a little too close to her boss. She'd "look out" for him and his business. She might be the one responsible for blowing the whistle at eight seconds, but might wait until nine seconds or just wait for you to get bucked off and *then* sound the horn. In an effort to kind of clean up things and make it more fair, Brian MacDonald, the bull riding director, initiated the rule requiring each of the two judges in the arena to have a stopwatch. Didn't matter if the whistle blew a second after you bucked off, if the judge's watch said eight seconds, you got a score. That was pretty neat because it helped quite a few bull riders and put an end to a lot of the underhanded stuff going on.

One particular week toward the end of the season in October 1980 I discovered I'd drawn an awesome set of bulls. I was scheduled to compete at four rodeos: Waco, Texas, on Wednesday, another one in Little Rock, Arkansas, on Thursday; Leesville, Louisiana, on Friday, and the last one in Texarkana, on Saturday. Texarkana is on the border of Texas and Arkansas, in the northeast corner of Texas. For the first time in my career, I'd drawn good enough bulls to win at every rodeo.

At Waco, I drew Bobby Steiner's bull, number 3-X, a black motley-faced horned bull I'd won on at the rodeo in Belton earlier in the year. That bull could buck! Right in the gate he turned back to the left, and kicked straight over his head. I made an excellent ride, but he tossed me off just as the whistle blew. The judge came over and showed me my time, which he did as a courtesy. It allowed a judge to explain to the rider, "Here's why I'm not scoring you."

I looked at the stopwatch. 7.83. I'll never forget it. 7.83. It broke my heart because that ride could've won the rodeo, and it would've paid between seventeen and eighteen hundred dollars. Plus, I was trying to qualify for the National Finals. Everybody told me I'd had a fantastic ride, put up super effort, just no score. "And," they said, "You rode a *great* bull." My spirit sagged, but I shrugged and said, "Oh, well. No big deal."

Well, I had to resurrect my morale, because the next night in Little Rock, I'd drawn JJ, a bull of Mike Cervi's. JJ'd pitched me off at Sheridan, Wyoming, so fast and hard I didn't care if I ever got up. I couldn't move. He bucked and spun right over the top of me. He knocked the breath out of me. In fact, he was so rank he knocked me silly. I thought if I could ride him *this* time, I'd win. I expected JJ might be the rankest bull I'd ride all week.

At Little Rock, I climbed on JJ. He turned back right in the gate, made a half-round to the left, and then reversed into my hand. Perfect for me! He went to the right and it felt like a superb ride. The fans screamed and hollered. The whistle blew. He bucked me off and as I fell he kicked me right in the back of the head with a POW! My hat flew up in the air. Everything seemed to happen at the very end.

Buddy Lytle, a fine judge who I have a lot or respect for, held the watch in his hand and came over to me. I was still lying on the ground. He put that stopwatch right down in my face. Although half-groggy, I could see it. *7.91.* Oh, no! Two nights in a row!

A friend of mine came over later and told me, "Terry, that's the greatest bull ride I've ever seen in my life. I can't believe you didn't get a score."

I shook my head. "I didn't get a score, man."

"But that was the best." He slapped me on the back. "You can really ride—good enough to go to the National Finals."

"Yeah, but I've gotta win some money or I ain't goin'."

At Leesville the next night, I drew a black bull belonging to Bradford Ivy, V-3. He was an excellent bull even though he fought the chute some. But a cowboy could win first on him, because not many bulls got ridden at this rodeo. This ride doesn't fit the way the rest of the story has gone, because he turned back right in the gate and threw me into the bucking chute. With or without a stopwatch, I rode this one about two seconds. I didn't get a seven-point-anything. Three up and three down. I'd planned to win every one of these rodeos, and these bulls all bucked fine enough that I could have. Talk about down in the dumps. I was discouraged and guess which bull I had ahead to finish off with and save my week?

Chapter 11

For Saturday night at Texarkana, I'd drawn 189, Jim Shoulder's bull, Double Trouble. Baddest one of the whole bunch. To top it off, no one had ridden Double Trouble long enough to get a score that year. He'd bucked off some highly skilled bull riders like Marvin Paul Shoulders (Jim's son), and Denny Flynn. He'd bucked off everyone who'd gotten on him and was in the running for bucking bull of the year. I'd drawn Double Trouble, and I was thrilled.

I watched a lot of outstanding bull riders ride that Saturday night. One of them, Lyle Sankey, had ridden Double Trouble a couple of years before. Lyle told me, "Terry, when I rode him, he went to the right. So be watchin' the right."

I thanked him for the advice and grumbled to myself about the bad week I'd had. I was supposed to have won every one of these rodeos. I decided I'd just finish it off here with Double Trouble.

I'd seen this bull before. When I was a junior in high school, Jim Shoulders put on a professional rodeo in Carthage. I entered as a hometown contestant. I'd ridden the bull I'd drawn, Crossfire 181, and was still in the money in sixth place. My friend Roy Carter, the final bull rider Saturday night, drew Double Trouble, rode him, scored 89 points, and won that rodeo, which kept me from winning any money.

I climbed on Double Trouble that night at Texarkana, took a wrap, and scooted to my rope. Lyle had said to watch for the right and sure enough, he turned to the *left* in the gate, bucking and spinning.

Of all the bulls I've ridden, I have to say, Double Trouble was one of the best two or three rides I ever made in my life. I scored 87 points. I'll never forget—my hero, Jim Shoulders, the stock contractor at the rodeo, owned that bull. He sat on his horse out in the arena during my ride. And even though I don't think he really knew who I was, him being there, shaking my hand, and telling me, "Great ride," made it even more special for me.

So I rode Double Trouble. The stopwatch for that ride must have made eight seconds, because the judge gave my score, the announcer called me a champion, and I won the rodeo.

I started the current season in second place, but early on fell to sixth. I sat at eighth place for a long time. Then I teetered on the edge at tenth place, then twelfth, fourteenth. I watched my dream fade away. My winnings became inconsistent.

Toward the end of the year I fractured my foot. I taped it and competed anyway.

The last rodeo of the season is always San Francisco. I had to win just a little something at San Francisco. To qualify for the National Finals Rodeo, I needed to score around 74 points to win enough to make the NFR.

I called the rodeo secretary from the hotel.

"This is Terry Holland. Could you tell me if I made the short go-round?" If I had, then it meant I'd go to NFR.

"No. Sorry, Terry. You had to have at least 74 points. You scored 72. You're one place out of it."

I'd missed it by two points!

Nobody loves rodeo as much as I do. This can't be happening. I gave everything I had and then some. Nobody cares or wants to win as bad as I do. This isn't happening. It rang in my head again and again.

So my season ended; no more rodeos. San Francisco had been my last shot to win or qualify for the NFR that year. I didn't make the top fifteen, and there was no way to move on up. That was it. The disappointment hurt worse than being stomped by a bull.

I came to realize there's a Y-93 in everybody's life. Sometimes a person draws that bull again and again. He dislocates a collarbone, hits you smack-dab in the middle of the nose, breaks your leg, or takes the little bit of money you have and leaves you empty, devastated, and alone in a San Francisco hotel room.

After frustration knocked me to my knees, reality seeped in. *Yes, it is happening.* And through the muddiness of loss, truth pierced my heart. *I love my work and it doesn't love me back. I need something that loves me whether I'm winning or losing.*

It dawned on me. *I've got it. And I've had it all along.* I'd accepted the Lord when I was sixteen.

I pawed through my rigging bag and pulled out the dusty, old Bible I'd tucked away. I began to study it and read about Jesus. I began to understand he's real and he loves me. I realized he wasn't asking me to quit rodeo, give up my dream, or stop being a cowboy.

Starting that day, I took him with me for the rest of my bull riding career and I continue to take him with me each day. Things became different from then on. More importantly, *I* was different. Even when I failed.

Early on in my career a guy from a Dallas area newspaper interviewed me about what I'd accomplished as young as I was. We'd done several stories about me and the bulls I'd ridden.

He said, "Terry, I need one more story to end this article that'll blow my readers away—right out of their socks."

I adjusted my cowboy hat and thought. "I did something pretty spectacular one time that we don't have in the article yet. I scored real high on a bull by the name of Double Trouble. I was the first guy to ever ride this bull. It was a big deal. How's that?" I said.

"Yeah, well, that's pretty good, Terry, but you know there're a lot of talented bull riders these days who ride bulls that have never been ridden. It's just not *that* big a deal. Isn't there something you can think of?" he asked.

"One time a friend and I were rodeoing over the Fourth of July when there're a lot of professional rodeos goin' on. We were trying to get to as many as we could, so we hired a pilot to fly us in a private plane. We rode in three different bull riding events in three different states in *one day*. We made it to about thirteen different rodeos in about six days." I thought that was pretty spectacular.

He frowned, shaking his head. "Nowadays, Terry, these modern cowboys do that a lot. Is there anything else we could end this article with that's just really impressive?"

I had one more story to try on him before I'd have to come up with something I didn't really do.

So I told him about one of the times I entered a rodeo in Texarkana.

The way professional rodeo is setup, you know which bull you've drawn before you even get there. In Texarkana, I was going to ride on a Saturday night and by about Tuesday of that week I already knew I'd drawn a bull by the name of Kung Fu. He was a great bull in his day. I'd actually ridden him once before and won on him, which gave me confidence. But the neat thing about drawing a bull you've ridden before is the thrill of riding him and the expectation of winning. Plus, he was sort of on the tail end of his career; he wasn't near as good as he used to be.

So I went up to Texarkana, got there early—unusual for me—and visited with one of the committee members who helped with the rodeo. A lot of times a Lions Club or a Rotary Club puts the rodeo on as a fundraiser. This committee member told me an interesting story, and I shared it with my interviewer.

The committee member said, "Terry, did you know that part of our arena is in Texas—actually about half of it—and the other half is in Arkansas?"

I shook my head. "No kiddin'?"

"On one end of the arena where you guys ride buckin' bulls and broncs, that's in Texas. The border between Texas and Arkansas goes right down the center of our arena. The other end, which is in Arkansas, is where they rope calves and have the steer wrestling event."

I decided it was kind of an unusual situation, but my thoughts focused on Kung Fu and my excitement about riding him again. Came time for the bull riding and as Kung Fu trotted in, I felt totally confident, thinking the secretary can go ahead and write that check out to me for first place. It's a cinch. It's a lock. A number of my rodeo friends knew I'd ridden him before and I figure they thought I was going to win the bull riding. I know they planned to do their very best, but *I* expected to win.

So I climbed up on Kung Fu, got ready, nodded my head, and they opened the gate.

The very first jump out of the chute this bull made me think, *I got myself on the wrong bull!*

The second jump, he was having the best day of *his* career. *This is way too much bull. He doesn't feel anything like the Kung Fu I rode once before!* With my arm completely extended, he already had me in a bad position, so stretched out I was looking straight up at the sky.

If you know anything about bull riding, you're supposed to be looking at the bull you're riding while you're riding him. I wasn't.

The third jump had me reaching what I call the point of no return. We parted company when he performed a violent, perfect, 180-degree turn in midair. He launched me like a rocket.

"And that's when I became the first man in history to get on a bull in Texas and get thrown plumb to another state, 'cause I landed in the middle of Arkansas."

I made it into the top twenty nationally in 1981, while rodeoing with Lee Newman. We entered a rodeo in Inglewood, California.

The bull I drew, 119, a white-faced red brindle Braford with straight horns, belonged to Cotton Rosser. I believed I could win on this bull, because someone had won a rodeo on him the week before.

Lee didn't draw a good bull so he turned it out and decided not to make the trip. A ticket from Texas to California meant a pretty big expense and when a cowboy entered a rodeo that far from home, he made doggone sure he had a chance to win before spending that much money. When you're rodeoing, it's hard to get a ticket two or three weeks in advance because you didn't always know where you were going to be or if you had a good enough bull to even make it worth going.

I didn't want to spend any more time than I had to in California, so I arrived out there about five p.m. The rodeo started at seven that evening and I had a ticket for the red-eye flight back to Texas at one-thirty a.m. This way, I didn't have the added expense of a hotel room and I needed to get back home to compete the next day.

The rodeo was held at The Forum, where the L.A. Lakers played. The cowboys' dressing room turned out to actually be in the locker room the Lakers used. Other cowboys had tied off their ropes to various lockers and started rosining their bull ropes. One of the available lockers had "Magic Johnson" over it. I thought this would be the coolest thing ever—I knew who he was! So I tied my bull rope to Magic's locker and rosined it right there.

I recall what bull 119 looked like. I remember getting on him, pulling my rope tight, and scooting up on my rope. I remember sitting on the bull and nodding my head. I don't know what happened afterward and nobody ever told me. I guess I'd been so addled I couldn't ask. Next thing I knew, I was in a hospital somewhere.

Bull 119 knocked me out, hooked and stomped, and hooked and stomped some more. Judging from all the sore places, he jerked me down and hit me in the head with his horn. I had a headache and a knot on my head. Every part of me ached. In addition to being sore all over, I didn't know where I was.

When I came to, I looked around and saw two guys standing nearby.

"Well, we're going to put him in a room," said the one who looked like a doctor.

"As I put away his equipment, I noticed he has an airline ticket in his bag. He's got a flight at one-thirty," said the other guy.

"We need to keep him. X-rays showed a broken collarbone, but…"

They looked over at me.

"Terry, are you awake?" the doctor asked.

"Yeah."

"Don't you have a flight?" he asked.

"Yeah, but I don't know when it is," I said.

The other man answered. "It's at one-thirty."

By this time it was about midnight.

"We'll release you, but just get checked out when you get back to Texas."

They whisked me out of that emergency room and into the man's car. On the way to the airport he told me his last name was Holland, too. Apparently, he came to watch the rodeo and after seeing me ride and get hurt, he thought I might need some help. He missed the rest of the rodeo and went along to the hospital with me.

"Man, I can't thank you enough. Um, I don't know which airline I'm on or anything."

"I can probably tell by looking at your ticket. Did you have other luggage?" He only knew about my rigging bag.

A little of my sense returned. "If I'm flying back on the red-eye, I didn't carry any other clothes. I was just going to ride and then be on that plane and headed back home."

I noticed people staring at me. I looked at myself and noticed my filthy, ripped-to-pieces "white" shirt. I didn't remember I'd injured my collar bone. When I picked up my bag, the pain reminded me.

Mr. Holland got me to the airport just in time. He walked me down to the gate and watched me get on the plane.

I slept on the flight back to Dallas-Fort Worth. Ricky Bolin, a cowboy friend of mine who'd been on the same flight, came up to me after we landed.

"Hey, Terry, are you doin' okay?"

"Yeah, I think I'm gonna be all right."

"Do you need any help?" he asked.

I slung my rigging bag over my good shoulder. "I think I'm okay."

"You sure?" he asked. "We're fixin' to take off."

"Honest, I'm okay."

Before he left would have been a good time to have said, "Man, Ricky, I don't know how I got here." But all I thought was, *Well, I made it here. I'm at DFW Airport. I'm okay.* I looked at my ticket and saw Dallas-Fort Worth as the destination. As I stood there, it dawned on me—I didn't know how I'd gotten there to begin with. *Did somebody drop me off here?* I walked over to the baggage claim area and sat on one of the benches.

I must be supposed to ride somewhere tonight. I knew I wouldn't be riding because of my broken collar bone. I called the rodeo event entry office, told them I'd been injured, and let them know that wherever I was supposed to ride, I wouldn't be there.

A thought occurred to me. *I drove my car here. But where did I park it?* I sat there for a long time wondering where I'd parked my car. Gradually it started coming back to me—*I drove here.* I dug through my rigging bag. I always put my watch, cash, and knife in one particular place. I opened the pocket and saw my keys. *Yeah, my car's here. I'm on to something. I have keys, but where did I park it?*

Even back then, DFW Airport was huge. I didn't know what to do. If I asked somebody for help, what good would it do me? *Did I park in the outer lot and ride the shuttle in? Did I pull up close because I was running late?* None of that information would come back to me.

I dug through my things again and saw a parking lot ticket in my billfold. I'd written where I'd parked on the stub. Fortunately, I had enough sense to go where it said. I got in my car and somehow made it home.

The Lord must have thought I needed more encouragement in my career because at this point, he brought Jay Horton across my path. Jay impacted my life and influenced me in a huge way..

Jay will be the first to tell you he never became a great bull rider, just an average one at best. He observed champion rodeo cowboys. He was probably the first guy I saw who wore starched 13MWZ Wrangler jeans with the brass brads on them. I was a little younger than Jay and, at the time, didn't know as much as he did. I watched him and learned how to dress like a real rodeo cowboy.

In spite of Jay's shortcomings he always stayed a dear friend and great encourager to me. Without a doubt, his gift is encouragement. He traveled with me to lots of the rodeos. One year he went along to Ft. Worth and watched me ride all four bulls there. I made the short round and ended up winning third in the whole rodeo. Jay went to every performance and filmed it with a little eight millimeter camera. I suspect he had to take off work to go with me, but he did it willingly, and with a servant's heart.

Jay sometimes entered the PRCA sanctioned rodeo in Carthage as a "hometown." There used to be a provision allowing contestants to enter local rodeos without having a permit or being a PRCA member. Participants just had to live within fifty miles of the rodeo location, in this case, Carthage, Texas. They did it that way in the old days to create a little interest so the local folks would come and watch a hometown participant. Now there are rules against it because of insurance issues.

Jay wasn't a big draw in that respect. He competed anyway and climbed on some of those great rank bulls, like Cyclone, and others belonging to Jim Shoulders. Jay rode but never did any good. He couldn't stay on. He still impressed me because he was a hometown guy, he knew how to dress like a cowboy, and he didn't hesitate to enter those events. And we've stayed in contact through the years.

I lived in a trailer near my arena in 1983. I kept bulls penned next to the arena and hosted jackpot bull rides on Monday nights. Twenty or more guys usually entered the event. Sometimes during the week, I'd hop on a couple of practice bulls. Most of the time I had excellent livestock around. Bradford Ivy, a local stock contractor, sent some of his bulls to me to help them gain some experience. The jackpot rides helped season them for future competition. But I climbed on some of the very best ones during the week instead of waiting for Monday night. Bradford felt confident in my ability to care for stock, plus I could tell him which ones bucked and keep him up on their progress.

Jay worked as a welder in our community and frequently came by in the evening. "You gonna get on bulls tonight?" he'd ask.

Most of the time, he'd just help out, watch me ride, and simply be an encouragement. I loved having him around. He never failed to tell me, "Terry, you're a fantastic rider!" He'd lie to me and I knew it, but his encouraging words still made me feel good.

He came by late one afternoon. "Are you gettin' on any of the practice bulls?" he asked.

"Yeah. I think I will. I have a rodeo comin' up."

He looked at the deepening dusk in the east. "Well, it's gettin' dark."

"Right before I get on, I'll have you run to the end of the arena and turn on the lights."

He nodded.

We put one of Bradford's best bulls in the chute. He'd sent over a big spotted one with huge horns—number 22.

Pretty for a bull, he had a lot of color and was tough to ride. He'd only been ridden a couple of times that whole year.

"Jay, it's getting pretty dark." Actually, it had gotten plumb dark. I couldn't see much of anything. "Scoot on down and flip the light switch while I rosin my rope and put on my spurs."

I heard Jay take off and expected lights in just a minute.

"What do you do to get 'em to come on?" he hollered.

"Just push that lever up."

I heard the lever clicking at the breaker box.

"They ain't comin' on," he said.

"You ain't doin' somethin' right," I said.

I found a flashlight and walked to the box. Two blown breakers. The lights wouldn't be coming on without some repair work first.

I stopped to evaluate the situation. This bull stood in the chute. All I had to do was put my rope around him.

"Ah, Terry. I was wantin' to see you ride that bull." Jay egged me on.

"I don't know about ridin' in the dark. Ain't done it before," I said.

"What difference does it make? You don't have to see much to ride him anyway."

"Well, you could be right. Might make a good story to tell the guys later." By the time we got back to the chute and I slid my rope on him, the sky had turned as black as pitch.

"Okay, Jay. I'm gettin' on him in the dark. You pull my rope and tighten the flank. You'll have to jump over to unlatch and open the gate. Then I'll ride him."

I climbed on 22. Jay pulled my rope and I rode that bull. He turned back and spun in the gate to the left. As he spun, I felt him drift away from the bucking chute and Jay, toward the middle of the arena. He covered ground as he drifted, which is worth a lot more points in competition because it makes a bull tougher to ride.

I could tell I was making an excellent ride. My spurs raked his hide and the bell clanked as I rode. Jay could only listen and strain into the darkness to try and see the spotted bull. Twenty-two didn't fight or try to run down the rider afterward, so we didn't have to worry about that.

I jumped off and hit the ground with a thud.

"Terry, that's the most fantastic ride I've ever seen in my entire life!" Jay immediately started in. "You have made one of the greatest rides ever."

I shook my head in the darkness and smiled. "Jay, it was pitch dark. You couldn't see *any*thing."

"Well, it *sounded* like the best ride I've ever seen in my life!"

Not long after my ride in the dark Jay came and entered the Monday night jackpot. He drew one of my best bulls from Bradford Ivy; number 45 had long horns that stuck straight up.

Sometimes Jay became kind of nervous and acted like he didn't want to ride. So I'd take on the role of encourager for him. "Jay, you can ride this bull," I told him. He made a great effort but still got thrown off. During his ride, the bull popped Jay on the side of the head. The blow didn't knock him out, only stunned him, but I checked on him anyway. "Are you okay?" I asked.

He rubbed a spot on his head. "I think I'm all right."

We finished the rest of the jackpot riding and then several of the guys jumped on a few practice bulls. I didn't think about Jay's injury again. Because he had to work early the next day, Jay usually left after he rode, especially when he bucked off and didn't win any money.

We finished up around ten that night. I noticed Jay sitting on his rigging bag, still hanging around after we were done. He'd put up his equipment already and seemed to be waiting for me. Gradually, everybody left. Like usual, I was the last one there, except for Jay. I turned the bulls into the different pens where they belonged.

Thinking he might be wanting to talk to me about something, I asked, "Jay, I'm through and the bulls are out, do you want to come up to the house?"

"Yeah, I think I will," he said. He grabbed his rigging bag and walked to the house with me.

Jay just kept hanging around. Soon the clock said eleven, then eleven-thirty. At quarter to twelve, we still weren't talking about anything important. I was supposed to catch a plane the next morning to head out to a rodeo and I needed to get some sleep.

Finally, I said, "Jay, don't you need to go home?"

He sighed. "Yeah. But, Terry, I don't remember where I live."

I stared at him. "What?"

He rubbed his temples. "My head hurts and I can't remember how to get home."

"You live in Tatum, Texas."

"How do I get there?"

"You're kiddin' me!"

He shook his head. "No. I ain't kiddin' you. I know who you are. I know I got hit in the head by a bull. But I do *not* remember where I live."

I drew him a little map on a scrap of paper and he managed to make it home.

Chapter 12

One August in the early 1980s, Ronnie Christian and I took off and made a little run to Kansas. During the month of August alone there are thirty-something rodeos in Kansas. He rode bareback broncs, and I rode bulls.

I liked rodeoing with Ronnie because he was a Christian. I thought it was funny that he's a Christian with the last name of Christian. He didn't drink, and I didn't have to worry about him getting in trouble or having something happen to him. Sometimes when you'd travel with other guys who lived a different lifestyle, you never knew what kind of trouble they might get into. The main worry was if you rode with them in their vehicle, and they were arrested, or lost their vehicle, there went your transportation, too.

We'd already competed at Hill City and Manhattan. Next on our list was the rodeo in Dodge City. We rented a hotel room there. We'd been rodeoing hard. Competing made us hungry and exhausted so we stopped for something to eat on the way back to the hotel. We rode down the highway in my Skylark and everything moved along fine. I loved that we were in Dodge City, Kansas. For me, it didn't get any more western than this!

We cruised down Wyatt Earp Street toward the downtown. We stopped in the left lane to wait on traffic so I could make a left across the oncoming lanes to get to our hotel. This stretch of road had no turning lane and I sat there with my blinker on, waiting.

Lots of vehicles came at us as we waited for a clear shot. Well, we waited and waited and Ronnie just chattered as we sat. I love ol' Ronnie. He's a good friend, but he can talk and talk and *talk*—which is great when you're driving, because he keeps you awake. I listened and watched the congestion as Ronnie yacked.

I'm a good, defensive driver. Sitting there made me antsy. *Someone's gonna hit me from behind.* "C'mon, c'mon, c'mon," I muttered.

Oncoming traffic streamed like a river. Cars zipped up and around us. I glanced in my rearview mirror and noticed a car coming up fast. I looked up again and blew the horn hoping to wake up the moron in the car about to hit us. I kept my foot on the brake.

There wasn't even time to warn Ronnie. I only knew cars on my right pulled around me and cars in a steady stream on my left came toward me. I couldn't turn. I thought the driver would pull over at the last instant until, BAM! A car smoked us, hitting so hard the bench seat in my Buick broke. It sounded like a fifty-five gallon drum falling off a house. That old Buick lurched forward with a jerk and took off down Wyatt Earp Street.

Looking back, I should have gassed it, but the car was probably going to hit us either way. We were protected because the impact didn't knock us into the oncoming traffic. Ronnie and I both fell backward, which probably saved us from breaking our necks. I looked over at Ronnie. We both lay in the back seat as the car rolled to a stop.

"Wh-what happened?" Ronnie asked.

"We just got rear-ended. You all right?"

"Yeah."

I climbed out and looked at my car. I walked around to the back. The impact folded and crunched the trunk. The trunk lid teetered and squeaked as it opened. Our gear and rigging bags seemed undamaged, but now the trunk wouldn't close. I looked at the seat where it lay flat, then back to the trunk. I felt sick about it.

Ronnie jumped out of the car. Worried about the woman who hit us, he went to help her. I walked back to Ronnie and the woman.

"Are you all right, ma'am?" he asked.

She climbed out of her car, looked at the damage on both vehicles, and covered her face with her hands. "I am *so* sorry."

Other people stopped and checked on us.

Come to find out, she'd been looking in parking lots for her teenage daughter who she suspected was out somewhere riding around town. The daughter hadn't called or come home when she was supposed to. Instead of looking at the road, the woman was looking for her wayward daughter. The police showed up. Her car had to be towed off.

"Will you need your car towed?" the officer asked me.

I shrugged. "I don't know yet, to be honest with you."

"Do you think it'll run?" he said.

"It's running right now!" I hadn't turned it off. I guess I'd put it in park and left it sitting there idling.

"Better see if any of your tires are rubbing."

The back of the front seat leaned into the floor space where someone would put their feet if they were sitting in the back seat. I climbed in, balanced myself on the broken seat, and put the Buick into 'drive.'

Ronnie watched as I eased forward and then backed up. Nothing dragged or scraped. The impact just mutilated my Buick's rear end.

"You guys need a place to stay?" the officer asked.

I pointed across the street to the hotel. "No. We're staying right there." We finally managed to cross the street and turn into the parking lot.

"Well, is that western enough for you, Ronnie?" I asked. "Here we are on Wyatt Earp Street in Dodge City, Kansas and we've been bushwacked from behind."

Even back then, you could sue someone for rear-ending you. Neither one of us wanted to do that. My Skylark looked like it'd starred in some of our rodeos. I just wanted it fixed.

But we still had more rodeos we'd planned to ride in. I wired the trunk lid shut. Somehow, we propped the seat partially upright with two-by-fours and rode low-rider-style to Phillipsburg, Kansas. Everyone wanted to know what happened, and we sure had a good story to tell.

That car saw some tough times and they weren't even my fault.

Debbie Jo and I drove from Carthage to a rodeo in Baton Rouge, Louisiana. I drew a good bull named Garfield. Back then, local groups like Rotary, Lion's Club, and Cattlemen's Association hosted rodeos to earn money for charity. At this event, committee members had the responsibility of opening and closing all the gates and chutes. They weren't cowboys, former or current rodeo competitors, or ranchers used to working with cattle. The gate men were volunteers—just some of the guys involved in the group—which made this event trickier than usual.

When a bull and rider are ready in the chute, the gate is opened just a crack at first, then real slow until the bull turns his head and starts to leave the chute. At this point, the gate is pulled out of the way and opened completely.

If a cowboy nods or shouts, "Outside," and the gate is swung open too fast, the bull is allowed to move forward and run down along the gate knocking off the rider.

That's just exactly what happened! I nodded. Without hesitation, the "gate man" swung it wide open. When Garfield jerked, it put me out of position and off my rope. He dragged me off toward the side coming out of the chute. I know it looked like I'd started to fall off, but that wasn't the situation.

The let-out gate turns the bull from the arena down the alley *after* the rider is either bucked off or jumps off on his own. Another committee man took care of this exit gate, but he didn't know what he was doing either. He opened the let-out gate prematurely —I wasn't off the bull yet, just tilting to the side and off center. Garfield came around the arena, saw the big gate begin to open, and in his anticipation, hit it as he jumped through.

That maneuver knocked me off the rest of the way, but my hand hung up in the bull rope long enough to pull me down underneath him. He bucked over me. One of his back feet came down on the side of my head and sliced through the bottom half of my ear.

Debbie Jo wiped off the blood and looked at it. "You really ought to get that sewed up."

I climbed on a bull at Nicky Wheeler's one night and the same thing happened as when I nearly had my ear torn off. This time the guy opening the gate knew his business, but this bull had a tendency to run down the gate anyway.

Double-Ought, a large tiger-striped bull with big ol' horns, would buck and spin right in the gate. I knew I'd drawn a good bull. I'd never seen him before, but I'd heard plenty about him. He'd been to a lot of amateur rodeos. Double-Ought always made a right-hand delivery, in other words, he made a right hand turn out of the bucking chute to enter into the arena.

The gate opener held the gate in the bull's face to force Double-Ought to turn his body. If he opened it just a little bit, the bull's habit was to hit the gate, fold it inside the arena, and then just lunge down it hitting the rider's leg on the way.

As Double-Ought shot down the gate, my foot snagged in the corner of the chute. The impact separated my foot and folded it completely around. Sometimes when you get injured like that the pain doesn't start until later. But this time the hurting had already begun. It pounded like someone had taken a hammer to it and I knew my foot and ankle had to be broken. He turned back to the left toward my injured side. *I'm hurt. I just need to get off.* My thoughts screamed at me.

We came around the corner of the chute. I rode one jump, then another. I spurred aggressively with my good foot. The whistle blew. *I'm in big trouble now! How am I gonna get off?*

I knew I'd be helpless and unable to run from Double-Ought once I managed to bail off. I had to depend on the bull fighter in the arena to do his job and to do it right. I hopped off as usual into my hand on the right side, and landed on my hands and knees. As fast as possible, I crawled away. Double-Ought didn't try to hook me or stomp on me and the bull fighters maneuvered him away. Three other guys had to come help me out of the arena.

I won the event with a mangled, messed up, painful foot.

The most interesting part was when we went to the orthopedic doctor in Shreveport, Louisiana. The injury amazed Dr. Burke. He gave me a brace and told me to stay off of the foot. Everything had snapped back into place, and despite some damaged ligaments, nothing needed a cast or surgery.

Dr. Burke said he'd seen my type of injury before in an orthopedic textbook. This same situation used to happen to soldiers in the Cavalry when they got shot, fell off, and had a boot catch in the stirrup. The foot would bend backwards the direction it wasn't designed to go. Thanks to me, Dr. Burke got to see a real example instead of just something from a previous era written about in a textbook.

At the end of the year the best bull riders in the world vote to choose that season's best bull. Number 124, Flying High never won best bucking bull of the year, but he stayed in the running and always seemed to come in second or third.

Bernice Johnson owned 124 when he first started his career as a rodeo bull. Bernice named him Flying High. Sponsorship deals came along and the very best bulls received names reflecting a sponsor. For example, if Black Velvet Whiskey sponsored him, the bull might be named Shades of Velvet. Sponsors paid stock owners well to name the animals that way. Even though sponsor money brought 124 a new name later, I've always known and referred to him as Flying High—one phenomenal bull.

In 1976, at Pretty Prairie, Kansas, Glenn Sullivan drew 124 Flying High while still a permit holder and long before he and I partnered up,. The first night 124 bucked off Nicky Wheeler. The next night he tossed Marvin Shoulders. According to those who saw it, Glenn made a fantastic ride the third performance and won the rodeo. He won a thousand dollars and earned his PRCA membership.

In 1977, Nicky Wheeler qualified and went to the NFR. Because he was an East Texas cowboy from Tyler, his accomplishment became big news, and we all kept up with how he did. At the NFR, a rider climbs on ten bulls, and Nicky rode nine out of the ten that year. Only 124 Flying High bucked him off.

In October, toward the end of the 1980 rodeo season, I drew Flying High at Liberty, Texas. Toward the end of our ride, as he bucked, Flying High kicked his leg through the fence by the chutes. He didn't seem to let it bother him because he kept right on bucking and ended up having an excellent day. I rode him, scored big, and won the rodeo.

As Flying High left the arena after I jumped off, his owner followed. "Something's wrong with him," he said.

I followed Bernice into the alley where someone pulled off the flank strap. Sure enough, I noticed the bull limping.

"I think he hurt himself, Terry." Concern covered his face.

I pulled off my hat and wiped a sleeve across my face. "Ah, man, Bernice. I'm sorry."

"It wasn't your fault. I'm not blamin' you. But I just want to watch him."

Bernice laid him off for nearly seven months. He planned to bring 124 Flying High back at the George Paul Invitational Bull Riding in Del Rio, Texas, in May of 1981. Flying High didn't buck from October 1980 until the following May.

As it turned out, I drew Flying High for the Invitational at Del Rio! I'd been the last to ride him the last time he bucked and the first cowboy to climb on him after he'd been declared well.

The national sponsor for this particular rodeo gave the current world champion bull rider a check for $30,000 to put into his account, which he got to keep only *if* he won all of the rodeos included in the promotional event. Donnie Gay happened to be the champion at the time. The sponsor designated thirty rodeos, including Del Rio, as part of this particular promotion. Donnie Gay got to keep $1,000 for each of those rodeos he won. If someone else won the rodeo, Donnie had to pay the winner an additional bonus of $1,000 from the money the sponsor placed into his account.

Flying High and I both must have been in good form because I made one of my best rides ever. I won rodeo prize money and the go-round that night, plus the additional amount from Don Gay.

I drew Flying High one final time in 1984 at the tail end of his career. I rode him again at Liberty, at the same rodeo where I'd ridden him in 1980, back when he was stronger and more rank. This time, I won third place with a score of 80.

Nine years is rare and a long time for a bull to buck professionally. Flying High—one exceptional, memorable bull that I rode and placed in the money all three times I climbed on him.

Debbie Jo and I were two weeks away from our first wedding anniversary in March of 1989. I was drawing good bulls, riding well, and had placed in the money at several rodeos. I'd won enough money that season to put me in the top twenty nationally and I flirted around in the top fifteen—those that go to the National Finals at the end of the year.

At the time, I tested cows as a livestock inspector for the state of Texas. This job suited my lifestyle well. I could go just about anywhere I wanted to compete for weekend rodeos, but if I ended up going to go to the NFR that year, it would come down to quitting my full-time job. It would be impossible to leave and stay gone the length of time I'd need to be away to qualify for and compete in the National Finals.

The success I'd had so far that season thrilled Deb and me. I'd just missed qualifying for NFR several times so far in my career. We thought maybe this time I'd finally make it. But in the back of my mind, conflict about possibly quitting my job pestered me.

I planned to participate in the Bay City, Texas, rodeo with two friends of mine—Virgil Wedgeworth, from Carthage, and Gene Stough, from Greenwood, Louisiana. They both drew excellent bulls.

I checked beforehand to find out which bull I'd drawn. Home Brew 65, owned by Bernice Johnson. I couldn't find out much about Home Brew other than he had a bad disposition, liked to fight, and would try to hook a rider once he got off.

Looking back, I made a poor professional decision. The bull I'd drawn didn't seem good enough to win on. I believe I would have turned out that bull if it hadn't been for my friends going, too. Deb and I decided to go anyway and make a little trip out of it, because we knew we'd have fun.

The three of us were scheduled to ride Friday night at Bay City and Saturday at two o'clock, in San Angelo, Texas.

C13 Top Cat. What a great bull! Sidney, Iowa, 1980. I rode Top Cat three times, the best of those in Nampa, Idaho, for 88 points. Photo by Ridley.

I'm attempting to ride the great 022 (of the Ivy Rodeo Company) at my home town rodeo. He got me off right after this picture was taken. I figure the flash from the camera was to blame.

Don Gay, me, and Roy Carter. Roy cost me placing at my first pro rodeo when he made one of the greatest rides I ever saw on Double Trouble (of Jim Shoulders). I finally got over it about 10 years later. Donnie cost me winning a bunch of times!

Hung Up to Ivy's 022 at Longview, Texas, 1982. Yeah, he's about to get me in the rear end. Photo by Denny Jernigan.

Chapter 13

When Debbie Jo and I began our cattle business, we leased about a hundred acres in Panola County, Texas, from Dr. Bush, a veterinarian and good friend, who worked for the state just like I did. He'd worked his whole professional life as a veterinarian for the state of Texas and retired in early March. I missed his party at the Animal Health Commission District office in Tyler because I had to test cows for a farmer.

One of the other folks I worked with called me. "You're not gonna believe what happened at that party!"

"What happened? What'd Dr. Bush say? Did he give a good speech?" I asked.

"No, man, he died." In the middle of his retirement party, he choked. It turned out to be an aneurism and he passed away at his retirement party.

Visitation for Dr. Bush took place at a funeral home in Garrison, Texas, which happened to be on the way to Bay City. Virgil, Deb, and I loaded up in Virgil's car and headed south toward Bay City by way of Garrison. We stopped at the funeral home, signed the register, and paid our respects to Dr. Bush, since we'd be missing the service.

We met up with Gene and his wife Lori, in Lufkin. Virgil left his car there, and we loaded our gear and ourselves into Gene's rodeo car—an old maroon four-door Buick with leg room and a big trunk.

Back in those days a lot of cowboys signed up to compete. The Bay City rodeo received so many entries, they had to divide the bull riding into two sections. I competed in the first section of bull riding.

As I asked around to find out who'd drawn Home Brew the night before, I smelled a rat. The judge's sheets were posted in the secretary's office. Ricky Lindsey (a National Finals bull rider) had drawn Home Brew for Thursday but didn't ride him. The sheet showed "visible injury release" beside Ricky's name.

At a professional rodeo, a rider can say he has an injury that hurts too bad to ride. A judge will take a look and if he feels it's legitimate, will grant the cowboy a release. A rider still has to pay the entry fee, but there's no fine like there is when stock is just turned out. I felt Ricky didn't ride Home Brew because he'd found out what a dud this bull was, not because of an injury. Ricky didn't like this kind of bull—nobody does.

I saw a number of friends when I arrived at the rodeo and took the opportunity to visit. Ron Conatser, one of the very first full-time cowboy preachers on the rodeo circuit, was one of the judges. An honest and fair judge, he refused to show partiality or favor to people he knew.

By the time I climbed on this bull, I'd gotten the scoop on him—he'll lunge straight down the arena, most likely won't turn back and spin and won't give me any chance to win. If he *does* turn and spin, it'll be too far down the arena. He's really dangerous and hard to get away from because he fights.

Since Virgil and Gene weren't scheduled to compete until the second section, they helped me get ready to ride. We kidded around and joked in an effort to relieve some of the pressure.

Home Brew probably weighed about nineteen hundred pounds—a big beast. I had no trouble riding him. He jumped around and kicked up a little but gave me no chance to win anything. I got off on the right side, just like I was supposed to. But his action wasn't strong enough to help me get away from him. When a rider steps off a bull that's really bucking hard, the bull will actually throw him clear. With the right momentum, the rider will land a good distance away, and on hands and knees, can get gone.

I landed right beside him. The instant I hit the ground and took a step to run behind and away from him, he kicked. As he came down, a back foot landed on my extended leg between the ankle and knee.

John Schuneman sat on his horse at the other end of the arena getting ready to steer wrestle. He said later he heard a sound like a .22 rifle going off, looked around and saw me.

I remember hearing that sound, too.

Sometimes when I rode bulls I didn't realize I'd been injured until later—after making it to the fence I'd discover broken ribs or a dislocated collar bone. My leg received such a blast, I had no doubt. I knew immediately I'd been hurt. Seriously hurt.

Don't stand up! This thought ran first through my head. Over my shoulder I saw the odd way my leg flopped. I knew it was broken and wouldn't hold me. *Stay put on your hands and knees,* I told myself.

Home Brew jogged to the let-out gate to leave the arena. The rodeo bull fighters did a good job of protecting me and had moved with the bull toward the gate. For some reason, Home Brew suddenly stopped, threw his head up, spun around, and looked straight at me. Here he came in my direction. By then, the bull fighters were out of position and couldn't help. It was just me and Home Brew.

I looked over and saw Snuffy Chancellor in his barrel. Most pro rodeos have a "barrel man" for audience entertainment and laughs. His main job is to help protect bull riders. I started crawling toward Snuffy. *I've got to get to that barrel.* I beat Home Brew to it and ducked in behind it. He didn't hit the barrel, just ran by very close, circled, and finally left the arena.

Gene Stough, not only my friend but a brother in the Lord, reached me first. I looked at him. "Gene, this is serious. I need you to pray for me, *now.*"

"Pray for what?" he asked.

"I don't know, just pray that I'll be healed and restored."

Ron Conatser, also a brother in Christ, put his hands on my shoulder and began to pray before the paramedics could even get there.

I've heard people say when someone breaks a leg, it's important to get the boot off quick as you can before the leg swells so big you can't *get* it off.

Another friend I'd rodeoed with for years arrived at my side with a pair of pliers in his hand. "Terry, I've got to get this spur undone to pull off your boot." The impact mashed my spur together, which was pinching my heel. He loosened the wire holding the spur down and removed it.

The paramedics prepared to cut open my boot and remove it when a man from the rodeo audience jumped the fence and ran across the arena. "Don't cut his boot off!" he hollered. "Do *not* cut that boot!" Nobody understood why he'd said that, but they left my boot alone. The man turned out to be a doctor who'd been watching the rodeo and saw what happened.

By now, the pain had started. Every time I moved even a tiny bit, waves of pain rocked me. I searched the stands, looking for Debbie Jo.

Chapter 14

Debbie Jo

I sat with Lori, Gene's wife, in the stands close to the bucking chutes when Terry rode Home Brew. As the audience applauded his ride, I heard a noise over the crowd but didn't know what it was or where it'd come from. I looked to the arena and saw Terry on his hands and knees moving toward Snuffy's barrel.

Instead of heading through the let-out gate, the bull circled around in the arena and came after Terry. Terry didn't stand, get up, and get out of the way like he normally would. He just crawled faster. I noticed one boot upright, while the other waggled and dragged through the dirt in an unnatural way.

"Lori, something's really wrong," I said. I made my way out of the stands and went to the side gate at the arena. I knew the rule—no one without a card is allowed into the arena. I didn't expect the men who worked the gates to stop me, but they did. They must have thought I'd be a detriment in the situation. They couldn't have known how much I've been around injuries and how desperately I needed to get to Terry and pray. I saw somebody hop the arena fence. *Well, that's just what I ought to do.* No one stood guard along the fenced section.

Both of the judges were out there. I knew Ron Conatser would be praying for Terry. The men in the arena crowded around Terry and blocked my view, but I saw someone motion for the gurney and ambulance. Normally, I'd be very angry that I wasn't allowed in, but this time I had a peace that it'd be okay without me. It seemed they were there forever.

The announcer's job is to keep the crowd interested and staying at the rodeo, and not let them be so offended by a cowboy's tragic injury that they're put off by the rodeo. This announcer talked constantly, trying to keep the audience engaged. "It's going to be awhile before the rodeo resumes, folks," he told the crowd. "Ladies and gentlemen, please be patient."

Terry

I stayed in the arena for a very long time. The EMS attendants stabilized the jagged bones sticking out of my leg as best they could. The splint's pressure made it hurt even more. They loaded me onto a stretcher. I felt every little bump as I bounced across the rough arena.

Man, this is worse than I thought. It's really bad.

In just a few hours I went from trying to decide whether I needed to quit my job to focus on trying to qualify for the National Finals, to a serious injury that could derail my life and career completely.

I remember thinking, *This rodeo season is over.* Competing in all the first-rate rodeos, having an excellent summer run, and possibly qualifying for the NFR had been in my plans. I expected to miss at least two or three months. April, May, June... And I *might* even have to miss the Cheyenne rodeo in July. Everything in my life suddenly froze as if someone had hit the "pause" button.

Debbie Jo

I stayed at the gate and watched as they brought Terry through on the stretcher. He looked pale and red with strain at the same time. He was filthy, dirt all over him.

Terry mumbled something to me I didn't understand. I figured he wanted me to come with him and turned to one of the paramedics. "I don't have a way to get to the hospital. We rode here with someone else."

"You can ride along in the ambulance," he said.

I glanced up and saw Gene and Virgil standing near me. "I don't know where we're going."

"Bay City only has one hospital," said the other paramedic.

Terry must have noticed his friends, because he mumbled through clenched teeth, "Y'all ride and I'll meet y'all there."

Events and time seemed to blur. We arrived at the hospital emergency entrance and a clerk met me at the door asking for information. She didn't understand I desperately needed to be with Terry in my role as rodeo wife and prayer warrior, because there wasn't anybody else. I wanted to rush in to Terry, but the clerk insisted I give her what she needed first. Finally, I felt I'd given her all the information I could. "Can you excuse me?" I pointed the direction Terry went. "Because if you need anything else, I'll just be in there."

I stepped into the exam room and noticed the nurses had removed his blood-filled boot and already cut open Terry's jeans. I stood next to the doctor and watched where the big light shined directly on Terry's leg. My eyes went straight to the mangled mess and two big doctor-hands pulling the fabric back and away from his wound. It looked a lot like a round roast with a bone in the middle—a large white bone and a lot of red meat, only jagged and covered with blood. Nothing fit together anymore.

The doctor bent over to explore bone and tissue.

I peered over his right shoulder and noticed an Aggie ring from Texas A & M on his finger. I looked over at him. "Neal Ware? What are you doing here?"

He looked back at me. "I work the emergency room here. Debbie Jo, what are *you* doing here?"

Neal had been an Animal Science classmate of mine at A & M when I first got to know him. I'd lost touch with him over the years and didn't know he'd changed professions.

"This man is my husband."

"What happened?"

"The bull stepped on him at the rodeo."

He nodded. "Compound fractures of tibia and fibula both."

"I don't know what you're thinking about or planning to do, but you need to know, he's going to want to continue with his rodeo career. He'll want to ride and use that leg. You've got to fix him." I tried to make Neal understand the importance of Terry being able to continue competing. Looking back, it probably sounded silly. I know they all hoped he'd at least be able to walk again.

He pointed to Terry's mangled leg. "This is extremely serious. We don't have the facilities to handle it here. Deb, I'm going to make some phone calls." Neal left.

It seemed like hours before Neal returned. "I think I'm getting something accomplished," he said. "I'm sending your husband to a trauma center in Houston where they can put him back together."

Terry

Neal hooked us up with the greatest doctors in Houston. As it turned out, Neal's godfather was Red Duke. Red was a well-known trauma doctor at Herman Hospital who had a television show about him. He had a big, red moustache and long hair, wore cowboy boots and a hat. I'd seen his television show and thought he was the coolest guy. We couldn't have gotten into Herman Hospital without Neal's help.

Virgil and Gene had asked if I wanted them to come to the hospital with me. I told them, "Ride your bulls first, then come check on me." They stayed and rode in the second section.

A broken leg. They'll line it up, put a cast on it. I'll be out for awhile, but it'll get better. I had no idea what I was up against.

Debbie Jo

If Terry wasn't delirious, he was awfully close to it. He talked, but didn't always make sense. He worried about his gear.

"Where's my riggin' bag? Did you get it?" he asked.

"No. I haven't seen it. Virgil or Gene probably got it," I said.

I thought they'd take Terry to Herman Hospital by helicopter, but his injury wasn't life-threatening, only limb-threatening. Terry's type of fracture involved great risk for nerve damage. He'd already been given all the morphine the hospital had on hand.

I turned to the nurse. "Do you have the information about where we're going? Our friends will be by here and they'll want to know where we are. Would you tell them to come there?"

The nurse gave Terry a fresh rolled-up cloth to bite and mopped his forehead. "Yes, ma'am. We will."

I had no other way to get to Houston, so they let me ride in front of the ambulance with the driver. I could tell he didn't especially want me up there with him, but we didn't have a choice. The ambulance driver tried to console me because I couldn't be in the back with Terry. The road to Houston from Bay City bumped the whole way. I asked the driver some complicated, technical medical questions.

"I really don't know," he said. "But I think he can be fixed. We're going to one of the best facilities in the country. I think he'll be fine."

Our conversation stopped. I wept in the darkness as we rode toward Houston. And, I prayed. *Please God, give me whatever it is I'm going to need.* I felt isolated, but not alone, strong yet weak, all at the same time. Such strange feelings overwhelmed me. I wondered what lay ahead of us. We'd only been married a year!

We arrived at Herman Hospital where the attendants unloaded Terry and wheeled him into the emergency room. People with serious burns lay on gurneys everywhere. The smell of charred flesh lingered in the air. In a little while, victims from a terrible multiple-motorcycle accident came past us. This wasn't our small hometown emergency room! This was big-city Houston, where injured and dying people screamed in pain and blood seemed to be going everywhere. I thought we were in desperate need and a high priority until I saw so many people literally fighting for their lives. Instead, I realized we were low on the totem pole. The hospital staff worked hard trying to get to everyone as fast as they could. There were so many.

Looking at the destruction and horror around us, I realized it could be bad, but it wasn't *this* bad!

They rolled us into a room with three curtained partitions and left us there. We stayed there long enough to get acquainted with other patients. One of them, a stabbing victim, sat up in a corner on a gurney as his blood seemed to squirt everywhere. "Hey, man. What happened to you?" he asked.

"Ridin' bulls" Terry mumbled. We didn't ask, but the man told us anyway.

"I was in a knife fight in a bar downtown," he said.

By now, I just knew Terry desperately needed more pain medication.

A young man and young woman showed up with a bucket. "We have to cast his leg to be able to x-ray it," he said. I stood nearby observing, while Terry was out of his head with the morphine. Two nurses stretched his leg beyond the edge of the table where he lay and started wrapping casting material around it. Part way through the process, they exchanged positions and as they did, one of the nurses dropped Terry's leg. It didn't bend at the knee but dangled at the fracture.

I sucked in a big breath and felt my eyes grow wide. I was afraid his leg would hit the floor.

"What?" he asked. The morphine had finally taken hold and he couldn't feel anything as they finished the cast.

I shook my head. "Nothing. It's okay."

The young woman turned toward me. "We'll be back. You need to go to the waiting room."

"Can't I go with him to the door of x-ray?" I asked.

She shook her head. "No, ma'am. You need to go to the waiting room."

I sighed. "Okay. Tell me where it is."

She gave me directions. I kissed Terry's head and mumbled something encouraging. Then they took him on the gurney and pushed it into an elevator. The doors squeezed shut.

Chapter 15

It seemed like I walked for miles to find the waiting area. Four houses the size of our home could have fit in this waiting "room." I couldn't see a single place to sit or stand. People were laid out everywhere. Children, having a grand time, ran and screamed throughout the area. In spite of their fun, a tragic, hopeless feeling permeated the space.

I must have looked like Scarlet O'Hara when she walked into the hospital to start taking care of those men as they lay dying and screaming for her help. I was appalled. Somehow in the chaos, I heard my name over the paging system. "Debbie Jo Holland, please come to the reception desk. Debbie Jo Holland." Thinking the clerk had news about Terry for me, I made my way through the crowd. There stood Virgil—a light in the darkness for me.

"Where are Gene and Lori?" I asked.

"They can stay if you want them to, but Gene's signed up to compete in San Angelo tonight," Virgil said.

"It's okay. They should go on and we'll catch up with them later." They'd decided if I didn't need them, Virgil would stay at the hospital and Gene and Lori would go on to San Angelo. Even with Virgil there, I felt so alone.

Virgil and I eventually located a place to sit and wait. About daylight, the receptionist paged me. Virgil walked with me to the desk.

A man came in. I could look into his eyes without having to look up very far.

"We're taking Terry to surgery. He'll be in a room afterward. I don't know exactly what we're going to do, but we're going to try and save his leg. I need your signature on this document in case we have to amputate his leg."

I know I blinked at him as if I hadn't heard him. In my brain, I stared at him for five minutes. I thought at the trauma center they'd put things back together, sew it up, and we'd go home. I certainly didn't expect this.

"Considering the location of his injury, I suspect vascular and neurological damage," he said.

"Okay." I sighed. "We're down here without a car. Our friends have already left. I need a timeframe so I can let someone know when they should come for us. That is, *if* you can tell me."

The doctor took me by the shoulder and looked me in the eye. "Mrs. Holland. We're going to try to save your husband's leg. I need you to sign here for possible amputation." He tried to hand me the clipboard and pen.

I ignored it. "What are you talking about?" I still had the impression they would fix his broken leg and we'd go home. "I have to *sign* for amputation? I don't think I can do that." I shook my head and sat back in my chair.

"Mrs. Holland, you need to. There could be vascular damage and it can't heal if we can't repair it. We don't want to have to go back in later."

"You don't understand! I've only been married to him for a year. I can't sign his leg away."

"I can't do the surgery without your signature."

"But I can't..." I stood and stared at him.

His voice became firm. "I can't do Terry's surgery otherwise." He offered the form again.

This time I took it. "Okay. I'll sign it." I used the clipboard and pointed it at him to emphasize my point. "But don't you *dare* take off his leg! You make sure he has his leg and can use it. I want it on straight and on good. I may be signing this, but I want good blood supply and full use of that leg. He's a young athlete. He's *got* to be restored. " My voice squeaked as I answered.

The doctor nodded. "We'll do all we can."

I looked at Virgil. His face mirrored the helplessness I felt.

I called Terry's dad. "Terry's kind of banged up and broken his leg. It's pretty serious."

"Do you need us to come?" he asked.

"I don't think so. They're taking him to surgery." This was all I could manage to say. "We'll call you back after he gets out."

Virgil and I sat for hours in a waiting room that seemed to go on for acres. We took turns trying to sleep. Finally, I went to the desk to ask about Terry and found he'd been assigned a room.

A nurse took us to Terry's room while he was still in surgery. Virgil and I sat in a pair of straight chairs and tried to make ourselves comfortable. Finding a place for his cowboy hat seemed to present a challenge to Virgil. He put his hat on his knee for awhile. Then he set it on his foot. He turned it upside down and placed it in his lap. The room didn't have a bed or anything to serve as a temporary hat rack. We continued to wait, talk, pray, and nap.

Finally, a nurse came in to let us know Terry was in recovery and doing well.

A little while later, orderlies wheeled Terry into the room. His leg looked like it had five-hundred pounds of stuff around it. Just being able to touch Terry made me feel grateful.

Terry

I woke up in my room after the first surgery to see Virgil trying to sleep sitting up in a chair. He left later that day, but I was thankful he'd stayed and supported Debbie Jo through the long wait while I was in surgery.

The doctor lined up the jagged edges and put screws through the bones, then attached an external fixator instead of a cast. They drilled holes in the top of my shin bone and ran screws through them—two above the fracture and two below it—then put two rods running parallel with the topside of my leg, attached to the screws. This allowed the doctor to adjust the tension to help my leg bones bond and heal.

The wound on my leg where the bones exploded through the flesh left a big hole. The muscle and flesh were torn to shreds. Part of my surgery included several debridements, where high pressure water removed the debris and dead tissue. It seemed I'd barely come out from under the anesthesia from one procedure before I would go back for another.

A nurse changed my dressings on a regular basis. My foot and leg felt heavier than normal after having so much water used to flush the area clean. When Home Brew broke my leg, he also severely sprained my ankle. The discomfort from the sprain seemed as bad as the pain from the fracture.

Then my heel started to hurt. I could tell something was wrong.

I'd developed a huge pressure sore on my heel from my leg staying continually in the same position. The pressure sore just added something else to treat and take care of. In addition to everything already going on, my abdomen began swelling and no one could figure out why. Finally, Debbie Jo discovered a kink in the tube of my catheter. She undid it and man, I got some relief!

After three debridement surgeries, the doctors decided they'd cleaned the wound as well as they could. A four-inch by six-inch gaping hole in my leg had no muscle or skin.

"We're going to need a certain amount of muscle and skin," the surgeon told me. "We'll get the skin from the side of your hip." They'd already settled on that location. "The muscle can come from either your stomach or your head, under your scalp."

The doctors let me make that decision. "I don't think there's enough under my scalp to do it," I said.

He nodded. "We can do it either way."

I had doubts about trying to recover from having my scalp ripped open. "Let's go for the stomach." I found out later taking muscle from my stomach was much worse than it would have been from my scalp.

The doctor sliced me open, pulled the skin up all the way to the bottom of my rib cage, and took out a piece of muscle from my abdominal wall. My scar looks like I had a C-section. Afterward I had staples from hip to hip and drainage tubes hanging from my chest. They also removed a chunk of skin off my hip, and went to work on repairing the hole in my leg. The doctor plugged the hole with that glob of muscle. They didn't take enough skin to fill the whole area; they cut it in perforated strips and layered it across the opening like lattice-crust over a pie.

So here I was, broken leg, sprained ankle, major pressure sore on my heel, *plus* a patch of skin taken from my hip and a hunk of muscle sliced out of my stomach. The area where they took the skin burned and hurt as much as my injuries. I had to stay rotated to one side and off of that hip. They kept a light shining on it and covered it with a big iodine-soaked bandage. As the bandage curled up along the edge, it was cut off. That patch on my hip ended up taking months to heal. I had a morphine pump for the pain. As soon as it would let me, I'd push the button for more. I developed an itchy rash all over my back, backside, and legs.

I thought I couldn't be any more miserable. To top it off, I had an unsympathetic nurse with the bedside manner of a rattlesnake. Things weren't all bad, though. Along with this cranky, unpleasant woman we had a wonderful nurse on another shift. She knew we were going through a tough time and treated us with kindness.

The stress almost pushed us over the edge. Debbie Jo and I cried together in misery. I apologized to Debbie for putting her through all this. Things didn't look good. But we looked to Jesus, stayed strong, and kept believing God could deliver me from this.

They kept checking my foot for circulation. Hospital personnel told me it wasn't a sure deal. We'd just have to wait and see. I still didn't know, and neither did they, whether or not I'd get to keep my leg.

Chapter 16

Debbie Jo

I had never seen Terry look so wild-eyed and behave like this before. I couldn't believe the person in the hospital bed was the same man I'd married.

He'd been put under so much anesthesia in such a short time he wasn't breathing properly. He just lay there. The nurses stayed after him about taking long, deep breaths at least once every hour to prevent pneumonia. They'd come into Terry's room, clap their hands, and almost shout, "Mr. Holland. Mr. Holland, wake up! You *have* to breathe."

He'd take in one breath as deep and loud as he could, exhale, and give them a mean, fire-eyed look. Then he'd go back to sleep. I don't think I've seen him as mad since, as he was when the nurses would wake him and make him breathe. He wasn't a very cooperative patient.

The itching became unbearable. Terry would roll to the side with his back toward me so I could scratch it for him.

The one thing Terry didn't want to happen was for someone to bump his leg. Afraid someone would touch it, he nearly had a fit anytime someone came near.

After several of the surgeries, one evening the famous Dr. Red Duke opened the door, strolled right in, and sat down on the bed by Terry's leg. I thought Terry would scream when Dr. Duke sat on the bed, but he didn't. I don't know if his leg actually would have hurt like before, but in *his* mind it hurt and he wouldn't even let me get close to it.

I remember watching Dr. Red Duke's medical segment on TV every night. He wore cowboy regalia and rode a beautiful horse through the snow.

Dr. Duke talked to Terry for a bit. He told him he thought things looked good and that he felt he'd continue to progress. "You have good doctors and they're going to take care of you. Our facilities here are excellent. And I think you're going to be able to get on your way. If you need anything, pardner, you just let me know."

It seemed to be an affirmation of healing, in spite of Terry having two more surgeries after that.

Even though family, friends, and rodeo people flooded us with calls and visits, I felt sad and lonesome. Terry looked so helpless and vulnerable. I began to cry. And we needed to cry, just the two of us. We prayed and cried together. I relied on my faith, not our circumstances. I knew God takes care of the sparrow and I knew he'd take care of us. There was nobody to rely on for our well-being and our future, except the Lord.

I stayed with Terry at the hospital for what turned out to be fifteen days. We'd planned to work the other rodeo and then come straight home. We hadn't expected to be gone for more than the weekend. You can imagine my grateful appreciation when several days into Terry's stay, two of my friends I'd known from A & M came by the hospital. They took care of me—we left the hospital and got some fresh air, talked about other things, went out to eat, and then they brought me back.

After one of the last surgeries, the doctor unwrapped Terry's leg. I wasn't ready for what I saw! His wound looked like a lattice-work cobbler. The doctor murmured something to the nurse about how good it looked. To me, it looked awful.

Terry

We had started a Bible study a few months back and those folks became prayer warriors for us. They'd call and ask, "What do you need?" After Deb shared our prayer needs with them, they'd tell others and we ended up with lots of people praying for us.

We learned the importance of letting people know specifically how to pray for us. For example, I couldn't sleep for three nights running. We relayed our situation to our prayer warriors. They prayed for me to sleep and sure enough, I did. Somehow, with lots of prayers, we dealt with all the itching, sweating, and more unbearable itching. I don't recall when we started to see progress. The thing I remember most was how terribly I itched and longed to take a bath. Sometimes in the middle of the night I'd ask Deb to help me get up and take a shower. Of course, that was impossible.

Home Brew 65 turned out to be a sorry dud and not only for me. Later that year, he broke Lane Frost's jaw. My score from the bull riding came back at 65—Home Brew's number. At that type of rodeo it usually took about an 87 to win and only the top six spots paid.

They finally released me from the hospital on our one-year wedding anniversary. I called my brother, Tim, and he drove down to pick us up. Going home was just the beginning of a lot of work for Deb and more pain for me. Debbie Jo had to clean my surgical wounds with peroxide, gauze, and cotton swabs at least three times a day. She had to rub the skin so it wouldn't grow onto the steel of the screws and fixator sticking out of my leg. Boy, that hurt.

Our community showed their care by the support they provided. People cooked for us and brought food. But along with the meals, we heard things like, "The Lord wants you to quit," and "You're not gonna let him ride those bulls any more, are you?" They didn't know Debbie had been praying that I could continue my career if it was what I wanted to do. When I look back, even wanting to ride bulls again seems absurd and ridiculous. I would have thought someone who'd gotten hurt in some sport would have learned a lesson. But I didn't believe the Lord wanted me to quit.

I climbed on a huge, mean bull and got off too close to him. My injury wasn't all the bull's fault. He kicked, stepped on me, and broke my leg. I believe God can protect me and I believe he had on many occasions. Riding bulls is an unnatural thing. It's also downright dangerous, very exciting, and something I did very well.

When I made it home, I still had a full time job working for the Texas Animal Health Commission, and here I'd broken my leg riding a bull—not working cows for the state. However, my state insurance covered all of it. After I'd used my accumulated sick leave and comp time, I still wasn't able to return to work, so I lost my job. Then things got really tough. There was a long period of time when I couldn't do anything and Debbie Jo had to take care of me. We continued to pray and believe God's plan included restoring me.

Even though we didn't know the name of the man at the rodeo who insisted I leave my boot on, God did. Deb swears he was an angel who flew over the fence and landed right there. God was already in control of a bad situation. Later, one of my doctors said that advice had probably helped save my leg.

We named the skin graft on the inside of my leg "The Glob." Everything had to remain open. It looked awful as it healed. I could tell it made people almost sick to see it! The Glob was kind of distracting and raunchy-looking, and people couldn't help but stare at it.

We went to see my surgeon, Dr. Melissinos, in Houston numerous times while my leg healed. One time while at the rehab clinic gym I met a man whose entire arm had been ripped off at the shoulder by the hydraulic lift on a garbage truck. They'd taken his arm out of the garbage truck and raced him with it to the hospital. The same doctor who'd done my surgery put his arm back on. I watched the doctor work rehab exercises with this man. The arm didn't look exactly like the one he'd been born with, but it worked and he could do a lot with it. Seeing this man's progress encouraged me. I started the rehab process and did what I was told.

We made another trip to Houston—this time to see Dr. Cotler, an orthopedic doctor. "Do you think I could get this thing off?" I pointed to my fixator.

"We'll have to see how it's doing, Terry."

I nodded. "Okay."

"If we think the bones have bonded and are doing well, we can remove the fixator and put your leg in a cast."

"That'd be great." I looked at Deb and smiled. There are some activities newlyweds enjoy that are really tough to do with metal screws and bars sticking out of your leg—like walking in the moonlight together.

About a month later we returned to Houston. "This thing is doing so well, I think I can remove the fixator." Dr. Cotler fiddled with the hardware and slid off the parallel bars.

Wow, he's taking it off.

With no comment, he went to work. He picked up what looked like an old fashioned brace and bit drill with a handle and crank on it. He fitted the tool on the head of the screw as we talked. He fiddled with the tool and I thought he was getting everything ready. Next thing I knew, he started cranking on that thing and backed the screw out of my shin bone while I sat there watching. Maybe he thought I was a tough cowboy, but I figured he'd either sedate me or numb my leg first.

Dark purple blood oozed out of the bone. I glared at him. "You should have said something!"

"I figured you wouldn't let me, if I'd said something first."

"You sorry outfit!"

Deb told me later the color had drained completely from my face. When she came over and put her hand on my back, she said it felt as hot as an oven.

He ran out the rest of the screws. We kept all the hardware—the screws and fixator pieces. We thought it was pretty cool, but the folks at the doctor's office thought Deb was crazy for wanting to keep them. After the doctor removed the fixator, he put my leg in a blue cast. We went back several weeks later for x-rays and had the cast removed. While I wondered if I needed another cast, the doctor grabbed my leg, put one hand above the fracture and one below it, and jerked on it as hard as he could. Then he called in one of the interns. "Feel this. Feel how strong it is."

She held my leg just like the doctor had and pulled on it.

I went across the street and they fitted me with a plastic brace that fit over The Glob. The skin and tissue took longer to heal than the bone did. We went from not knowing if I'd keep my leg to realizing we were going to make it. I could walk even though it took a long time before I could put my leg down for more than a moment without feeling it would explode from the pressure.

At therapy they told me not to limp. "Do not let yourself learn to limp." So I didn't. Getting the cast off felt good and I progressed along all the way to being able to take a shower.

We really needed some income. The PRCA was good to me and while I still wore the plastic brace, they let me judge a few rodeos.

The whole time I recuperated I planned a comeback because quitting after I'd gotten hurt would have been something I would have had to live with for the rest of my life. I didn't want to do that. If I hadn't been physically able to continue, obviously I'd have quit. I made the decision to ride bulls again but wondered how long I should wait.

One of the first rodeos of the season is Odessa, Texas, the first week in January. After getting released by my doctors in October, I set the Odessa rodeo as my goal. This gave me about three months to get ready. Deb understood and supported me, but it was hard on the rest of my family; they'd been thinking I would finally quit.

Chapter 17

The prospect of getting back on a bull scared me. I'd been practicing and staying in shape by using my bucking barrel—the Mighty Bucky prototype I'd made—but it wasn't the real deal. Close to Christmas, Norman, a local bull rider friend, and I decided I needed to get on a practice bull before the rodeo. A friend of Norman's owned some bulls and he let us come out and ride.

The bull I climbed on crashed into the fence as he bucked and hit my right leg. That crash worried me. *Oh, man. Surely I haven't messed it up.* Thankfully, my leg wasn't re-injured and I went on to compete at Odessa.

At the Odessa rodeo I drew a huge black white-faced bull that probably weighed a ton. One hundred and five bull riders entered. I came in fourth and placed in the money my very first ride back. It really felt good! Debbie Jo and I praised God for his restoring touch. Wow, what an adventure.

Looking back, I could have been prone to regret that rodeo in Bay City. Debbie Jo and I grew so close. Going through that valley with the Lord made our walk with him so strong. I've never said I wished I hadn't gotten on that bull. I know it sounds crazy—it was extremely painful. We went through a terrible season, but there's no way we can say it didn't make us better people.

When I talk to kids about riding bulls I tell them: "Until you overcome a severe injury, then come back to compete and have some success, you haven't experienced bull riding. The only way you're going to understand is to go through it."

It's like Donnie Gay says about bull riding, "It's not a question of whether or not you're gonna get hurt, it's when and how bad." It may not make the paper or even the rodeo sports news, but you're going to break something sometime.

In 1992, The Christian Broadcasting Network (CBN) filmed the story of how I broke my leg and the testimony of how God restored me. It ran several times on *The 700 Club*.

As a result, a number of people called the program and made decisions for Christ. Our walk through the fire gave Debbie Jo and me a story to share and to impact others for God's Kingdom.

At the rodeo in Mesquite one evening, most of the participating bull riders were unknown to the audience. Near the stock pens at the end of the stands is a chain-link area with a small counter for signing autographs. Before the bull riding started, the arena director asked me to stay after my event to sign autographs.

"Yeah. No problem," I said.

I rode a big brindle bull. He turned back and bucked me off so fast I didn't know what happened. I hit the ground. He hooked me, ran over me, and threw me into the chutes. "Sore" described my state of body and mind. I put my equipment away.

"What happened, Terry?" A television reporter shoved her microphone in my direction.

"I'm basically embarrassed. I didn't ride well at all. If I'd ridden him and jumped off on my feet like I'm capable of, none of this would have happened."

The arena director walked by about then. "Terry, as quick as you can, go sign autographs."

I sure didn't feel like doing it even though I said I would. Rodeo fans are like tourists. They want an autograph from a real bull rider, and they don't care who it is. Each year I signed something different, like "God Bless" or "Keep your eyes on Jesus."

This particular time, as fans handed me a photo, I'd ask whose name to put on it, scrawl the name, then write, "Look to Jesus. Terry Holland." Much of the time, I didn't even look up as I wrote.

"What's your name?" I asked the next person in line.

"Emily."

A woman instead of the usual male fan.

I wrote, "Emily. Look to Jesus. Terry Holland." And I handed her the picture.

Finally, all the fans who wanted an autograph drifted away with mine in hand. I still felt aggravated and out of sorts at my earlier lack of success.

A couple of weeks later, I received an envelope from the Mesquite Rodeo. *Maybe I placed in something and didn't pick up my money?* Inside was a letter sent to the Mesquite Rodeo, addressed to me. It said, "I was contemplating suicide. Someone insisted going to the rodeo would cheer me up and make me happy and everything would be okay. I knew deep down that it wouldn't, but I went anyway. When you wrote 'Look to Jesus,' you gave me the answer. All I needed was hope—in Jesus."

What if I'd told the arena director, "I'm sore. I'm hurting. Get somebody else."

What if he'd turned to another bull rider and said, "Hey, Joe. Will you sign autographs? Terry doesn't feel like it."

What if Joe had gone to the booth instead of me, signed photos with his name and written, "Hang tough," or "Best wishes, Joe."

When I felt like a total failure and didn't feel like signing autographs, it wasn't about me at all. It was about writing "Look to Jesus" on a picture.

This girl was desperate for a sign of hope from God. A simple message, the power of the name of Jesus, saved someone's life. And God used a sore, discouraged cowboy to deliver it!

In 1990, Longview, Texas, hosted a PRCA rodeo and by then, I'd begun limiting competition to only those rodeos I wanted to compete in. I entered this one because Longview is close to home.

I called to find out which bull I'd drawn. Wouldn't you know it, I drew Skoal's Outlaw Willie, one of the most ornery bulls around. He belonged to Sammy Andrews, a real good bull man from northeast Texas. Sammy also owned the famous bull Bodacious. Although he purchased Outlaw Willie out of amateur stock, this bull had already created a legend because of his rankness and ability to buck. An athletic black bull with no horns, Outlaw Willie went to the National Finals.

I felt good about drawing a competitive bull and knew I could win this event by making a great ride. Getting on Outlaw Willie turned out to be a problem. He squatted and leaned. He pushed against the backside of the chute trying to get the advantage. We messed with him a long time in the chute, which is not good. I prefer getting on, tightening my rope, scooting up there, and nodding. But in this case, I couldn't because Outlaw Willie refused to cooperate.

Finally, I managed to maneuver myself into a pretty good position. I nodded. Outlaw Willie spun to the left in the gate and bucked me off so quick I didn't even make it out of the chute. He tossed me from the bucking chute into the arena. I hit the ground on hands and knees.

Usually, after he threw off a rider, Outlaw Willie made a little circle, bucked his way down the arena, and left. He didn't have a habit of trying to hurt anyone or chasing after a cowboy. The bull fighter knew Outlaw Willie wasn't mean, and he stood nearby waiting for the bull to head to the let-out gate.

I glanced over my shoulder and crawled as fast as I could when I saw him right behind me. I knew he wouldn't try to stomp me on purpose, but he headed directly toward me, still bucking and kicking as he moved away from the chutes. He snorted, spooked, and jumped. As his back legs kicked straight to the sky, he walked over me with his front feet. I felt his movement as he came by, pushed me and seemed to go on past. But his weight and momentum came down on me with his back feet. His hoof scraped the side of my neck along my ear, then BAM! He stepped on my jaw! It felt like a telephone pole dropped from the top of that arena had hit me.

I slumped into the dirt. If he'd been three inches over in one direction I'd have died because the impact would have exploded my head like a melon. He could have broken my neck or crushed my chest. If he'd come down three inches the other way, he wouldn't have even touched me, and we would have laughed about it later. Breaking my jaw sounds bad, but I called it a miracle.

My friend Rusty ran into the arena to me. "Terry, you all right?"

"That bull knocked my teeth out." I felt a gap in my mouth about the width of two teeth. I felt a little pain but nothing severe. "Where are they?"

Rusty shook his head. "Maybe they're in your mouth."

By then, people swarmed the arena trying to help me. They dug around in the dirt looking for my missing teeth.

I put my tongue in the space and didn't want to believe it. "My teeth are gone!"

One of the paramedics reached me. He looked at my face. "You broke your jaw and it's just hanging down."

A jaw cannot break in just one spot. The way it's designed, it's going to break in at least two places. Mine broke in three. Still, I worried about my teeth! I was bummed out. It hadn't been that long since I'd broken my leg and had to stay out for ten months.

They took me to a Longview hospital where surgeons put my jaw back together with plates and screws. They used bands instead of wire to immobilize my jaw.

Because the rodeo took place close to home, lots of my friends had come to see me ride. I returned from surgery to a roomful of folks visiting, talking, and having a good time.

I slept off and on for a couple of hours. Deb told me while they waited for me to come around, they'd turned the TV to a channel that played old Western shows. All of a sudden, my eyes popped open and I noticed the television. "High Chapa-dadgum-ral's on!"

They laughed at how silly I sounded. Of course, no one could understand what I'd said because my jaw was locked in position.

Two weeks later I actually competed in a rodeo with my jaw still banded shut.

Several people told me I'd lose a lot of weight and get weak while I healed. I set out to prove them wrong. We had a blender and Deb ground up most any kind of food. We'd go to Daddy Sam's Barbecue and get my favorite things— chopped beef, sausage, beans, then pour that tasty sauce over it and pre-chew it into soup with the blender. I'd stick the straw into the side of my mouth and suck down my meals. I "ate" milkshakes, too. When I went back to the hospital to have the bands taken off they weighed me. I'd gained seven pounds since the surgery. Most people with immobilized jaws dry up and blow away. Not this cowboy!

Chapter 18

Back in the early 1990s, as a committee member, I helped with the PRCA rodeo in Carthage, Texas. They had a good funny bull fighter/rodeo clown, but something wild needed to happen. I bought a gorilla suit at a costume shop. I wrote out a routine for the announcer so he could follow along and we performed our little skit for fans in Carthage.

Our skit worked out well because the events included two rounds of bull riding, one at the first part of the rodeo, and then another at the end. Both sessions included excellent, competitive stock. Usually, they'd put the best up for the first session so everyone would get thrown off. Our skit came after the first round of bull riding and toward the end of the show but before the second round.

Then we loaded a special bull in the bucking chute. And I hid out in the back wearing my gorilla suit.

"I know y'all are disappointed with the bull riding in the first section," the clown said. "Nobody stayed on. That's why I brought my go-rilla Clyde with me tonight."

"Your what?" asked the announcer.

"That's right. I've got a bull ridin' go-rilla."

Everybody in the crowd chuckled.

"You got a gorilla that rides bulls?"

"I guarantee ya, I got a go-rilla and he can ride better than those guys did."

"I don't know," the announcer said. "These guys are professional bull riders. They're the best in the business. You expect us to believe you got a gorilla that can ride a bull? You're crazy. Get out of here, and let's get on with the rodeo."

"Wait just a minute." The clown shook his finger at the announcer. "I'll bet you my go-rilla can ride one of these bulls."

The announcer and clown made a bet.

"I'll be right back." The clown ran out and brought me in on a leash.

I'd practiced beforehand acting like a gorilla. I ran around all humped over and dug in the dirt. Plus, I had a *good* costume. I wore gorilla feet with big rubber toes that slipped over my tennis shoes. I had black gorilla hands, too.

All those old cowboys laughed. They didn't know for certain who was wearing that costume, and they probably wondered if the gorilla would really climb on a bull.

I brought my own for the skit—a huge tiger-striped brindle with big horns. I couldn't wear spurs to get a hold on him, so I had to ride a bull I was used to. I knew he'd buck, and I figured I could ride him.

We set it up to make it look like the second session of bull riding was about to start. A cowboy named Tommy sat on a bull, heating up his rope. He actually sat on the one I was about to ride, heating the rosin on *my* rope. We didn't tell anyone but Tommy what we'd planned. I tore loose from the clown and headed toward the chute.

"Which bull is he gonna ride?" the announcer asked.

"Which ever one he wants to," the clown replied. "He's gonna pick one out."

I went up and down the chutes sniffing the stock, kicking up dirt, getting after people. The guys ran from me. I came to the chute where the cowboy sat on my pre-selected bull, number 72.

"Wait. He can't ride that one," the announcer said. "Tommy drew that bull and he's getting ready to ride it. It's his."

"Well. I bet he's fixin' to get off," the clown nodded and smiled.

I climbed up the chute, jumped on the top, and swung a little bit. I grabbed the cowboy's hat and tossed it.

He took off running.

I hopped on the bull.

"Well, I guess he's really gonna do it. Ladies and gentlemen, y'all want to see a gorilla ride?"

The crowd went crazy and gave the gorilla a standing ovation. Just what our rodeo needed.

While pulling my rope, I grunted and woofed loud enough for the audience to hear. I tightened the rope and scooted up.

Man, now I've really got to bear down if I'm gonna stay on.

That gorilla head wobbled around on my head and I couldn't see that well through the eye holes. The gate opened and I rode him eight seconds. The horn sounded. I bailed off and the people went wild. I swung my bull rope around over my head and threw it into the arena.

Several years later I ran into a young lady who'd seen our skit that night with her children. She told me when she saw me walking into the arena on a leash behind the clown, she told her kids, "Lord, have mercy. I hope he doesn't get in the stands. That's a *real* gorilla."

We went to a rodeo in Edna, Texas, in the mid-1990s when my daughter Khakie Jo was still a baby. The bull I'd drawn, though known for being tough to get away from, would buck and give a cowboy a good ride.

I rode, heard the whistle. A qualified ride. As I prepared to bail off, Miles Hare, one of the greatest bull fighters ever, hollered at me. "Wait a minute, Terry."

I realized Miles wanted me to wait until he could get the bull turning to the left. Then I could dismount to the right, which would give me a better position to get away. Miles knew from prior experience how cagey this bull could be.

When he bucked in a tight little circle to the right, I could tell he'd done this before. The bull sensed from the way I prepared to bail off that I was right handed. Smart old bulls just have a way of knowing those things.

I waited, kept riding, and waited some more.

The bull stayed in that little circle turning to the right. Miles hadn't given me the word to bail off, but as the bull jumped forward, I went anyway. Before I hit the ground, his horn hooked me, and I landed underneath him. I tried to cover my head and crawl at the same time. I couldn't see what was happening. He seemed to be dancing on top of me and every direction I tried I either ran into his legs or he stepped on me. After one of his horns delivered a hard blow to my head, I heard a loud ringing sound in my ear. Thankfully, it didn't knock me out. He mashed my face into the dust with his head. The misery seemed to go on forever.

Miles finally grabbed him by the horn and gained his attention. The bull picked Miles up and tried to hook him, which gave me the chance to skedaddle.

I went to the local hospital for stitches. I hurt all over. I couldn't ride the next night in Corpus Christi. I'd usually just cowboy up and go anyhow. This time I hurt too bad to be tough. I got a doctor's release for my injury and turned out the bull. Like I always say, "It ain't ridin' bulls that's dangerous; it's gettin' off!"

Chapter 19

The year 1996 brought an opportunity to help a good friend. Billy Jaynes supplied livestock for PRCA rodeos mostly in Texas. As a contractor, he also provided stock for quite a few of the small town rodeos. Debbie, Khakie Jo, and I used to go to them because Billy and his wife were our friends and sometimes I competed.

It wasn't easy getting people to come out to those small town rodeos because they didn't always have top-ranked contestants. I tried to think of a way to make Billy's rodeos better. We decided they needed a "little something." I told him about my stint as a gorilla in Carthage, just to give him some ideas.

"That didn't cost a thing," I told him. "It's not like those acts that are twenty-five hundred dollars a night."

"Will you do it?" he asked.

That wasn't why I told him about it. I just wanted him to see he needed something similar. I didn't answer right away.

"Aw, man. C'mon. Do it one time!" Billy said.

"Okay, I'll do it once. I want to use my own bull." I had a big black banana-horned bull. "Banana horns," also called scurs, looked like two loose bananas hanging down and swinging from his head. Scurs are gray colored and hard like regular horns but have no base. A lot of times if you cross polled cattle like Angus, with cows that have horns, you'll come up with something in between.

For Billy's rodeo I did my act with Snuffy Chancellor, the bull fighter whose barrel I'd crawled behind when Home Brew broke my leg. Snuffy always hammed it up. Billy loved the act. I ended up agreeing to perform at his rodeos for the whole season.

Our act started with Snuffy bringing me in. I played around in the dirt and ran all over the arena like a gorilla. I ran to the corner, dug a little hole, and acted like I used the bathroom, then covered it up. Sometimes Snuffy brought me in through the stands. After making my initial appearance, I ran off and hid.

"Where's he at?" the announcer asked.

Snuffy shrugged and went out the gate to look for me. Then he came back into the arena shaking his head. "I can't find him."

"Can't find him?" the announcer said.

"Uh, I got some bad news. He's done got loose," said Snuffy.

The audience hollered and women screamed.

"Where do you think he went?"

"Well, when this usually happens..."

"You mean this has happened before?"

"Yeah. When it usually happens, well, I find him up in the stands." Snuffy pointed toward the audience.

About then I swung up and over the back of the stands then woofed and grunted on my way through the bleachers to the arena. I tried not to scare any little kids. But I got a big kick out of watching grown men spill their drinks, fall, and cuss at me when I woofed in their ear from behind or pulled on their pants. The women always screamed even louder than they did to begin with.

Christian recording artist Crystal Lyons sang at some of Billy's rodeos. She could ride and sing on horseback. She gave an outstanding concert and sang the National Anthem, too. Billy had Crystal casually walk across the arena. Her long blonde hair hung down her back. I'd spot her and go to strutting or acting silly.

"Uh oh. Uh oh," Snuffy said.

"What's the matter, Snuffy?" the announcer asked.

"I didn't know there were gonna be any women around. This is a womanizing ol' go-rilla."

I followed Crystal around and looked at her, obviously impressed by her.

"If he hurts Crystal Lyons, you're in big trouble." The announcer said.

"He won't hurt her. She just needs to be perfectly still," Snuffy said.

"Crystal, if you don't move, he won't hurt you," assured the announcer. "Trust me. If you won't run from him, you're fine."

Crystal acted scared.

"Whatever he wants to do just let him do it."

The crowd laughed.

I peered at Crystal, walked around her, stared at her hair, then acted like I was picking bugs from her hair and eating them.

People went crazy and almost fell out of the stands laughing. Some made disgusted sounds.

After pretending to eat a few morsels, I ran off.

"I think he's ready," Snuffy said.

We basically had the same setup as before—a cowboy sitting on the bull as though preparing to ride but really heating my rope for me. I'd run him off and then ride the bull. I did it a bunch of times and never got bucked off. I *had* to ride! I had to stay on or it would have ruined the act.

Toward the end of the season we performed at Humble, Texas. As I often did, I rode as a competitor in the first session, then did my gorilla act. I had my black banana-horned bull ready in the chute with my bull rope on him. The boy who pulled my rope knew how to adjust it perfectly. I couldn't go up there and adjust it myself. It'd look fishy.

We went along in our act and came to the part where I would go to the chutes. I couldn't see real well with that gorilla head on, so I looked for the chute with a guy sitting on my bull. This time I saw a guy sitting on a big brindle with horns that stuck up.

Uh, oh. Those horns don't belong to my bull! They're up to something. But we were in the middle of our act. I woofed at Billy. Sure enough, they'd left my black banana-horned bull back in the pen and ran this brindle through instead.

Well, I can either go through with it or not. This bull had been in the draw. He was a *real* bull, not one I knew and felt comfortable riding. Well, I figured if he bucked me off, that'd be okay; the gorilla had to go down sometime. So I climbed on. He bucked, jumped, and kicked. I managed to stay on and ride him.

"Don't y'all ever do that again!" I scolded them afterward.

The guys all laughed. Some cowboys who didn't know what was going on told me later they thought Snuffy just had a professional bull rider who traveled with him, dressed up as a gorilla, and rode for a jump or two, then bailed off.

I stomped someone's cowboy hat every act. Most of the time, I got the guy who flanked for the riders. I'd grab his hat, stomp on it, and throw it away. Then the guys who worked the gates became part of the act, and they'd put on old hats instead of their good ones. David, whose cowboy hat I stomped regularly, worked for Billy. He and the guys in the chutes decided they'd play one on me by running this brindle in there instead of my banana-horned bull.

One of the last places we performed our act was at Kingsville, Texas, home of the famous King Ranch.

I started doing a victory dance after my gorilla rides, similar to one Dion Sanders did. He danced, spun, threw his hands up, lay back, and fell in the end zone. Usually, way out in the middle of the arena, I did a little dance, leaned back, and fell like I'd been shot. When I hit the ground, the act was over and I'd skedaddle on out.

The black bull bucked pretty hard this particular time and for some reason, he circled right around in front of the bucking chutes instead of going straight like he usually did. The whistle blew and I jumped off.

"I guess he showed y'all. My go-rilla rides better than some of them cowboys," Snuffy hollered.

The crowd went crazy. The music started, and I went into my victory dance.

The bull made a circle. Justin had responsibility for the gate. He kept his eye on the bull and tried to get him to come around while keeping me from getting run over. Ready to let the bull out, Justin pushed the gate and let it swing open slowly.

With my back toward him, I went into the falling part at the end of my victory dance. As the big pipe gate swung out bit by bit, I leaned with all my weight and fell backward. The back of my head hit that steel pipe on the bottom corner where the pipe forms an angle. A loud bonging sound rang out.

My head busted open inside the gorilla mask and the impact knocked me out. I lay there while the audience screamed and laughed thinking it was part of the act. I lay there until Billy, in the arena, hollered, "This gorilla needs a doctor."

Some of the cowboys and paramedics ran out to the arena to see about me. A couple of the guys helped me to my feet and I made a wobbly "gorilla run" out of the arena. Blood ran down the inside of my costume. Behind the chutes, a paramedic took a quick look under my mask. "You'll need stitches," he said. "But it's not life-threatening."

"Good. No use paying for an ambulance ride when it ain't necessary," I said.

After my act, the kids usually hunted for me to see the gorilla close-up. In my addled state I couldn't think and didn't need the attention of my young fans right then.

By the time the paramedic finished checking my head, Deb had made her way from the stands to see about me. She and two of the cowboys lead me away from the arena area. We stopped at a closed door.

"What's in here?" Deb turned the knob and discovered a storage closet. The two of us stepped inside to hide me until the rodeo finished up.

I pulled off the mask so she could get a better look at my wound. After Deb helped me out of the rest of my costume, I made a trip to the hospital to get the gash in my head sewn up.

Because I have a relationship with Jesus Christ, I pray about everything related to my ranch and business. I started raising bucking bulls on my ranch toward the end of my career. In the early 1990s, I had a set of gorgeous tiger-striped brindle two-year-old bulls for sale.

My friend, Donnie Gay was in the stock contracting business at the time. As I prayed about selling them, I felt he needed to own those boys.

I called him. "Donnie, I've got twenty-four of the best, good-looking bulls on my ranch, just like those your daddy used to buy."

"I'd love to have them, Terry, but I ain't got any money. The stock contracting business has been a little rough. I just don't have the money to do it."

"You've got to come take a look, or I'll send you a video tape of them. I feel like you're supposed to have them."

"Oh, no. Don't send me a tape, then I'll want 'em. I don't even want to see 'em. I just can't do it."

Another stock contractor called, ready to buy my bulls for the price I wanted. I needed to sell them, needed some cash flow. But I felt so strongly about Donnie owning those bulls, I tried one more little plan.

Donnie contracted to supply the stock for a rodeo nearby in Jacksonville, Texas.

Several days later, I loaded eight of my best looking bulls in the trailer and hauled them to Jacksonville. While Donnie talked with the secretary in the office, I pulled up to the pens, backed the trailer around, and kicked the bulls off into the alleyway. They looked so good.

Pretty soon, Donnie Gay came be-bopping out of the secretary's office. Some of his hands stood by the rail pointing at the bulls. I could tell they were drooling—and why not? These bulls were magazine ad material—big and beautiful. Donnie walked to the fence and looked them over. "I should have known you were gonna trick me." He adjusted his ball cap and looked up at me sideways.

"Well, what do you think?" I asked, leaning on the gate.

"Man, I love 'em." He watched them stir around the pen. "I'll have to borrow the money, but I'll take 'em."

"We're in business. I've got twenty-four in all. There's one black bull in there that I love. The rest are tiger-striped. Tell you what, I'll take a little pressure off you and keep the black one." I pointed toward the bulls.

"Naw, that's my favorite. I want him. I want 'em all." He shook his head and grinned.

So I delivered them all to Donnie Gay's ranch.

The rankest bull I ever got on was Mr. T. This photo was taken in 1987 in Odessa, Texas. I almost rode him (7.2 seconds) and if I had, it would have made me the first guy to ride him. But it would be 1989 before Marty Stanert finally twisted him at Cheyenne, the same day Lane Frost was killed.

Here I'm riding T13 of the Steiner Rodeo Company at Waco, Texas, 1978. I'd seen Nicky Wheeler and Don Gay ride this bull so I was a little nervous but successful. Photo by: Huffman Foto.

Winning second at Lufkin, Texas, in 1982 on a Steiner Rodeo Company bull. Check out the mud.

No bull was more feared by bull riders than Bernice Johnson's 88. Terry Walls, 88's former owner, called him Jaw Breaker for good reason. Looking on from inside the arena L to R: Tim Meador, Darrel Barron, Monty "Hawkeye" Henson, Ricky Bolin, Don Gay and Skipper Voss. Photo by: Al Long, Granbury, Texas.

Wrangler Bull Fighting and Bull Riding Invitational. Oklahoma City, Oklahoma 1980. Bull Fighters: Miles Hare, Skipper Voss, Rick Chapman, Rick Young, and Wick Peth. Bull Riders: Andy Taylor, Ricky Bolin, Dan Lowry, Randy Magers, Terry Holland, Wacey Cathey. Photo by: Huffman Foto.

Liberty, Texas, 1979. I won fourth place for this ride on bull #13 owned by Bernice Johnson. After I dismounted, he jumped out of the arena and headed down the middle of the carnival. When cowboys finally roped him, he had a stuffed toy monkey hanging from his left horn. Photo by: Huffman Foto.

Here at the old Mesquite Arena in 1978, I'm riding Black Smoke as a permit holder. NFR bull rider and good friend, Ricky Bolin, who was injured at the time, is judging from the fence where he appears to be right behind Black Smoke. Photo by: McShan

Here I'm winning third place at the Don Gay Classic at the Reunion Arena in Dallas, Texas, 1981. Only the top 16 bull riders in the world were invited to compete. Photo by: Huffman Foto.

Chapter 20

Back before the laws changed about tobacco advertising, one of the biggest rodeo sponsors was Copenhagen Skoal. If a bull went to any championship and his name contained reference to the tobacco company or related activity, the owners received extra money from the sponsors.

Now, the Gay family is funny about naming their bulls—they don't name one until he does something to earn it. A few months later, Donnie and I hosted a bull riding school, and he brought "his" bulls for use in the school. I asked if he'd named any of them yet.

"Well, yeah," Donnie pulled his ball cap off, then set it back on his head.

"Which one?"

"That black one."

"Why?"

"He's just special, Terry. There's something about him, so I named him after my favorite Dallas Cowboys' player, Dion Sanders. Dion's nick name is Prime Time, so I named the bull after him."

"Well, I hope he bucks."

"Actually..." Donnie shot me a sly grin. "I named the bull Skoal's Prime Time."

Now some of the bulls I sold him bucked at the school, some didn't. Prime Time's turn came. He stood perfectly still, never fought the chute.

When the chute opened Prime Time bucked and turned back to the left. He took to it so well the first time, I believe he was the rankest green bull I've ever seen in my life. We almost had to get oxygen for Donnie Gay! I'd just judged the PBR in Albuquerque and someone could have won by five points riding this bull. He outranked everything.

I kept up with Prime Time for several years while I continued my career and he ended up going to the pro-rodeos. Every once in awhile I'd see him, although I didn't draw him.

Donnie called one day. "Ol' Prime Time bucked Royd Doyle off."

I was impressed. "Really? Royd rides good. Real good." I felt like a proud parent with a football star for a son.

"He'll buck. He's fancy. He's fine."

I continued to keep up with Prime Time and saw him on occasion. Donnie had been right—Prime Time really was something special. He became a champion bucking bull during his career.

I'd ridden bulls for quite a few years at a professional level. Along about 1994 or so, I realized if I rode through the 1997 season, I would have ridden bulls twenty straight years in the Professional Rodeo Cowboys Association (PRCA). And I was riding competitively, winning money, not just hanging around.

There aren't many records, but I began checking around to find only a handful of people had competed for nearly that many years in a row. Even the outstanding long-career bull rider Freckles Brown, missed a whole year because of injury. Others took time from their careers to serve in the war. Bull riding in the PRCA for twenty consecutive years just hadn't been done. So that's what I decided to aim for.

At Fort Worth, over the years, cowboys carved their names into the wood behind the bucking chutes. My name included. I'd been there recently and noticed the carvings were gone. I hope when the arena was redone someone thought to preserve that particular slab of cowboy rodeo history.

In 1997, my bull riding career began coming to an end and I wondered, *Where will the last rodeo I'm ever going to ride in take place?* I'd already decided the 1997 season would be my last, but I hadn't made an official announcement. This would be *it*—the end. Bull riding had been all I'd ever done and all I'd wanted to do since I was five years old.

For the past two decades I'd ridden in the great rodeos across Texas and the rest of the country. This last time around I acknowledged at each one, *I'll never be here at this rodeo again.* This became a real emotional time for me.

In April of 1997, I entered a rodeo in Corpus Christi, Texas. I was scheduled to compete on Friday night. For Saturday evening, I planned to speak at a Stonecroft Ministries meeting in the area.

I drew Lightning, one of the bulls in the bunch with Prime Time that I sold to Don Gay. Don and his brother Pete both told me how well Lightning bucked.

I heard another cowboy had ridden Lightning the first night of the rodeo and scored 82. Drawing a good bull excited me and I looked forward to riding him.

Friday evening I climbed on Lightning, took a wrap, scooted up, and nodded. The gate opened. But the bull didn't turn back in the gate and spin like he had the first night. He made it tough to stay on by bucking straight and hard, really getting it on. Lightning came to the bull fighter's barrel in the middle of the arena. It looked to me like he was going to butt it. Instead, Lightning tried to jump it. As he did, his back legs hung up on the barrel and made him stumble. Seven seconds into the ride, he tossed me off. Our momentum drove me into the dirt where I landed on my right shoulder.

On my way out of the arena I moved my right arm; or I should say, *tried* to. Not only would it not move, it hurt. *Man, I must have dislocated my shoulder or something.*

Behind the stands the paramedics looked me over. "You broke your collar bone pretty bad," one of them said.

I felt sick. No one can ride with a broken collar bone. You can be as tough a cowboy as you want to be, but the collar bone holds your dad-gum shoulder in place. To make matters worse, I broke it on the right side—my *riding* side.

I wasn't just injured physically, but emotionally bruised as well. This injury crushed me like a sledge hammer. I knew I'd miss many of those good summer rodeos that year— Cheyenne, Salinas, Salt Lake City—and as it turned out, I didn't get to ride again until the middle of August.

Debbie Jo and I spent much of the night in a local hospital emergency room. A doctor put me in a brace that pulled both shoulders back.

I certainly didn't feel like going to any kind of meeting the next night, but I'd agreed to speak for Stonecroft Ministries, so I went. Several people accepted Christ that evening. In the middle of it all, God honored my obedience and willingness to serve even though I'd been injured and felt awful.

This injury kept me out for around four months. A cowboy doesn't come back and ride bulls right away after getting hurt like that, even if he wants to. And I couldn't back up and change my mind about retirement because of an injury.

I trained on my Mighty Bucky simulator, but didn't ride any real bulls because I didn't want to risk jarring and possibly re-fracturing my collarbone. When I came back in August, the season was almost over. September and October mark the end of the year for bull riding.

After working hard to get in shape, I entered a few rodeos. I rode a muley brindle bull at Grand Prairie, fell off, and embarrassed myself. Pitiful. This wasn't how I wanted to finish my career. I wanted to retire with a little competence and dignity. I didn't want people to say, "Man, Terry, you *need* to quit."

I got on a few more bulls, rode them okay and had a little success, but I was rusty. Thirty-eight is old for riding bulls. I'd only been on seven or eight bulls the entire year.

I wanted to retire at one of Don Gay's rodeos because I'd been to his school when I was a kid and he'd bought those bulls from me. Don had sold his rodeo company, was moving on with his life, and would no longer be stock contracting. I thought, *Wouldn't it be great to retire at one of his rodeos and draw one of the bulls I raised?* It didn't have to be Prime Time, but a perfect bull like One-Thirty. He'd hop and spin. I didn't expect to win first place, but third or fourth would do just fine for my last ride.

I entered the upcoming Rusk County PRCA rodeo in Henderson, Texas. Another rodeo Don Gay produced was still going on in Texarkana the week before the Henderson event.

Glenn Sullivan, who'd been judging the Texarkana rodeo, called. "Terry, I think I've seen the rankest bull I've seen in a long time. This Prime Time you sold Don Gay is bad news. He just jerked Scott Breding down and broke his jaw."

He barely took a breath before adding, "Another **PBR** rider had him the next time and rode him about two seconds. A kid from Florida had him one night and only rode him one point eight seconds. This dude is just bad news!"

Sunday after the Texarkana rodeo, Donnie Gay called and left a message on my machine. "Terry, ol' Prime Time really bucks. He's goin' to NFR!" He went on to list the riders Prime Time bucked off. No one had ridden him for eight seconds. Donnie was proud. As quick as he could, he wanted me to know I'd raised a bull with a reputation that was going all the way to the National Finals Rodeo.

The next day as I mowed some pasture at the ranch on my tractor, my wife, Debbie Jo, drove out in the pick up. "Have you called to find out which bull you've drawn for the rodeo in Henderson?" she asked.

"Naw, I haven't. Since Donnie's supplyin' stock, I just figure I'll draw one of the bulls I sold him. Don't know which one." I cleared my throat, adjusted my cap, and wiped the sweat off my forehead. "I might pick this rodeo as my last because it's about the last one Don Gay's going to put on."

Debbie Jo just looked at me in silence, tears forming in her eyes.

I could tell she hadn't expected this rodeo to be my last. "You know I've been thinkin' about it and just hadn't picked a particular time yet. You call for me, Debbie Jo."

She picked up the mobile phone and called. She gave them my card number, which is required to get through. "C15615L. Terry Holland's entered in the bull riding, Henderson, Texas. Which bull does he have?"

Debbie Jo turned a pasty shade of white. "Would you say that again?"

Chapter 21

I took the phone from her. "Hello."

"Is this Terry Holland?"

"Yes, sir."

"I have you in the third performance. Your stock is number one twenty-nine..." He could have stopped right there.

"Skoal's Prime Time."

"Thanks." I turned to Debbie Jo, feeling giddy and nervous.

Her face remained pale, but she tried to smile. "How 'bout that?"

"That's great, awesome. All right." I gave a weak laugh intended to give us both a boost of confidence.

Debbie headed to the house, and I crawled back up on the tractor and sat there. I thought, *Oh man, I just heard how he'd nearly knocked a couple of cowboys' heads off. And I can't ride like I used to. What am I gonna do?* I wasn't scared, I was horrified.

I played a possible scene through my mind. *Ride Saturday night, win the rodeo, then retire.* I knew too much. I knew who could and who couldn't win, and on a bull like Prime Time, only the very best even had a shot. A very slight shot at that.

Well, here's a deal, this'll work—*I'll get on him, try hard, and he'll buck me off and I'll retire, bucked off a bull I raised.* That'd be pretty good, to get on my last bull and I can't ride him because he's so rank. I could be satisfied with that.

Tractor in gear, mower whirring, I began to pray. Sometimes we think we have a plan. How we think, isn't always how God thinks. As I prayed, I played out for him the various possibilities for my last ride, as if the Lord needed to see the different ways it could go.

"I ain't much of a rider now—I'm thirty-eight. I'm old. Lord, I don't believe I can do this." I thought of all the

negative stuff. "Oh God, I don't know what to do." I ran the
tractor for about an hour and a half more before he began to
show me. I started to feel some confidence, then to believe
maybe I could.

Looking back, it was absolutely ridiculous to think at my
age, as rusty as I was, that I could ride this bull.

"Tell you what, let me play with this a little more." I told
God. "I wonder what shirt I'm supposed to wear? How 'bout
one of my Mighty Bucky shirts?"

The Lord began to show me which shirt to wear. I can't
explain it, I told Debbie Jo later, but I'm supposed to wear
my very best King Ranch white shirt. They're real expensive
dress shirts. I get them for Christmas; I don't buy them for
myself. I'd never worn one to ride a bull because it'd get stuff
on it Deb wouldn't be able to get out.

"So, God, which hat should I wear?"

The Lord impressed upon me to wear my brand new,
$450, 20X black hat. Normally, I'd never wear it for bull
riding, because sometimes I fell on my head and I didn't
want to mess up my good hat! Didn't matter. He impressed
upon me to wear my best, so I would.

"And do you have a suggestion on my jeans, too?" I
hoped I didn't sound presumptuous, but I wanted to know.
Back when I began my career every cowboy wore 13MWZ
cowboy cut Wranglers, designed specifically for professional
cowboys like Jim Shoulders, Pete and Donnie Gay, and
Larry Mahan. Many cowboys including me had started
wearing the comfortable, loose fit style of jeans for riding. It
came to me clearly, *Wear what you started with.* I had one
new pair of 13MWZs, and I was to wear them.

Then I realized I'd bought a new rope, though why, I
didn't know. It had never been used and was in my rigging
bag. I wanted to use my old bull rope. It felt good,
comfortable, worn—maybe too worn, with a little movement
in it like you're not supposed to have. The Lord impressed
upon me to use my new rope!

"Whoa. Lord, I'll wear my new hat and my white dress
shirt. I'll wear the 13MWZ jeans. But I don't know about
using a brand new bull rope on Prime Time." Every time I
thought about using the old rope, I felt weird. So I gave in.

"Oh, all right." I put it on a Mighty Bucky and practiced with it several times during the week before the rodeo.

Deb and I went to the Henderson rodeo on Thursday night to "case the joint" and watch Prime Time. He stomped one of those cowboys, wiped him out. Boy, that didn't help my confidence! Maybe I should have stayed home instead.

While we were there I saw Donnie Gay. "Donnie, come here a minute."

"Hey, you got ol' Prime Time, huh? You got a plan?" A smile creased his face.

I shook my head. "No." And I didn't. "This is going to be the last bull I get on."

His grin disappeared. "Really?"

"Yeah. I told you this would be my last season and I've decided this rodeo is my last. That's it." There it was, out in the open and spoken. I'd said it.

Donnie tipped the brim of his cowboy hat up off his forehead. "Well, okay." He nodded, as if he understood.

I had called several of my friends and told them of my upcoming retirement. One call went to Glenn Sullivan, the judge at Texarkana who'd seen Prime Time and told me how bad he was.

"Glenn, buddy, come pull my rope Saturday night."

"Why? What's the deal?" I sensed his hesitation.

"I'm retiring. It's my last bull."

Because Glenn and I go way back and traveled together to countless rodeos across the country and around Texas, I wanted him to pull my rope for my last ride. Many times during our careers we "pulled the rope" for each other in preparation for a bull ride.

"All right, Terry, I'll be there for you. I'm honored. What'd you get?"

"Ol' Prime Time."

"Oh, Terry." The way his voice dropped told me he was concerned although he didn't say so.

Glenn told me much later he felt sorry for me when I'd told him I'd drawn Prime Time. He hated to see me go out like that. Other friends shared Glenn's thoughts.

Glenn is a good Christian guy and he began to pray. At first he didn't think I could ride Prime Time. But as the week ended, his thinking changed from "no way could Terry ride

Prime Time" to "Terry just might could do it one more time."
Glenn would know probably better than anyone, because
he'd seen me ride some rank bulls during my career.

On Saturday Debbie, Khakie Jo, and I went to
Henderson for the rodeo. Deb and Khakie rode in the Grand
Entry in front of a first-time-in-history, sell-out crowd. Don't
know if they came because they'd heard I was retiring or just
because they enjoyed rodeo. People everywhere. Folks who
knew me took videos and photos, made a big deal out of it,
and asked dozens of questions.

"Hey, Terry, this is it, really?"

"Whatcha gonna do now?"

"No kiddin', you're retirin'?"

"Debbie Jo, is it true?"

The busyness and commotion began to get under my
skin. *I've gotta get away from this.* I turned to leave, but
just then Donnie walked up and laid a hand on my arm.

"Terry, you're gonna ride at the end tonight. Saturday
night, the final performance, you'll be the last bull rider to
ride. It'll be something real special."

I didn't know what to say. In my heart, I'd hoped for a
little recognition for the length of my career and passage to
retirement but didn't really expect it to happen. I must have
looked dazed because he added, "Hey. Wake up! Look at
me." The urgency in his voice cut through the crowd's noise.
"Here's what I want you to do."

Oh, here comes the advice, I thought. *But heck, he's the
only eight time bull riding champion in the world. He's
entitled to give me a little advice!*

"For me, ride him one jump. That's all I want, Terry.
Ride Prime Time perfect for *one* jump." He patted me on the
back and walked away.

I thought a moment about what he'd said. We've taught a
lot of schools together. We tell students when they get on a
rank bull, if everything ain't going perfect the first jump,
they will not ride him. The bull will have his day. Donnie
knew what he was doing. He had told me the one thing I
needed to know and planted the thought in my head—*ride
perfect for one jump.*

Chapter 22

I found a quieter spot away from the lighted arena, past the chutes and pens, way out back beyond where the barrel racers would come in for their event. Shutting out the rodeo sounds, I sat on a bale of hay. Filled with anxiety and an urgency to be honest with the Lord, I prayed and wept. "Lord, I ain't sure I can do this. I don't want to disappoint my family and the friends here cheering me on, but I ain't sure I can do this."

"Well, Terry. What do you need?"

"The body of a twenty-year-old would be nice," I said. "I rode good when I was twenty. I'd just like to believe I could do it again—I need to believe I can."

"Then you need the faith of a child."

The Bible talks a lot about the faith of a child. Why does a child have so much faith? Because it's blind faith. It's like a little eight-year-old boy who thinks he can ride Andy Capp, a rank bull, and he can't. It's physically and humanly impossible. But my childlike faith at age eight said I could. I was positive. No doubts.

"Well, Lord. I'll take the body of a twenty-year-old right quick, and the faith of a child." While I sat and continued to pray, I looked outside into the darkness.

Now, y'all, I'm not into a lot of weird stuff, but this is true. As I peered into the darkness, my life flashed before me like it was on a video screen. I could see any part of my life perfectly clear. I watched myself ride a calf and my bucking barrel. I fast forwarded to when I broke my leg really bad in Bay City, Texas, and Debbie and I had only been married a year. I lingered at each scene and watched it happen. I saw myself riding bulls at Houston, Denver, Fort Worth. My life unfolded before my eyes. No lie! I saw it. A lot of people believe me, because I'm a cowboy and a rancher. They think, surely a person like me couldn't make up anything goofy like that. I'm telling y'all, it was a *special* night.

Now, why would a guy's life play like a movie before his eyes? The answer flashed through my mind before I could stop it—*because he's going to die?* I shook my head in defiance and returned to watching my life.

I enjoyed the "video" so much I didn't want to leave, but with the barrel racing going strong, I knew it was time. "Thank you, Lord. I gotta go. I'm fixin' to give my best effort." God knew what I needed.

I strode toward the arena and saw Prime Time spinning around in the holding area leading into the chutes. The sight of him gave me goose bumps. A couple of other bulls bucked, and then in he came.

My sweaty hands trembled as I pulled out my new bull rope.This simple act of preparing to ride Prime Time became real emotional for me. I removed my cowboy hat and used my sleeve to wipe away the sweat trickling down my face. I've climbed onto about fifteen hundred bulls during my professional career—not counting those I sneaked around to ride.

This is the last bull I'm ever gonna ride.

As I readied my rope around Prime Time, my heart pounding, I recalled how many times I'd tried to put my rope on so I wouldn't have to adjust it. Almost a game, I would look at the bull and guess how big he was to know where to place my rope.

My bull rope went around Prime Time. I pulled it tight, then loosened it off. I started to wheel it around and adjust it just for the heck of it anyway, but found I didn't need to. It was perfect, exactly perfect. I'd put my rope on no ordinary rodeo bucking bull, y'all!

For the last time in my career—in my life—I took the tail of the bull rope, tied it off, and stuck it underneath the handhold like I'd done more than a thousand times. I left it there, got down, and went over behind the chutes to listen to the rodeo and savor its familiar smells—hot dogs, popcorn, manure, livestock, and sweat.

"The leader in the bull riding is Tuff Hedeman with a score of eighty-three," said Randy, one of the announcers. The crowd clapped and hollered in response.

I'd pulled Tuff's rope for him Thursday night when he rode a bull I raised.

Randy continued, "Terry, indeed, is a good friend of mine. He's taught some of the great talents you see today in the sport of bull riding.

"As a matter of fact, he's moving from one arena to another. He's now a rancher with his beautiful wife, Debbie Jo and their young daughter, Khakie Jo. He raises bucking bulls, so it's ironic and fitting tonight, by the luck of the draw, he drew a bull he raised and sold to Don Gay.

"Now here's a more interesting story. Terry Holland will tell you this bull is probably one of the most outstanding young athletes that have come off the Holland ranch. He's only been ridden two times in two years. Well, we'll find out."

The suspense, tension, and excitement inside me grew as Randy talked on.

"Terry Holland. Charles and I could go on and on about the talent. Twenty plus years as a PRCA member. He's been in the top twenty a half-dozen times. Just missed qualifying for the National Finals Rodeo by one position. In that career, he qualified in the Texas Circuit Finals and has won the Mesquite Championship rodeo as well. He's the only individual besides Don's brother Pete, who's helped instruct Don Gay's Bull Riding School for the past half-dozen years, and Donnie has used some of his bulls to do so.

"It's an honor to see this man here, I wanna tell ya. A thirty-eight-year-old veteran bull rider. Let's get behind him and see if we can't get this thing done the right way tonight."

Applause and cheers thundered throughout the arena.

All chutes except Prime Time's stood empty. He waited in the back chute on the left hand delivery side. Somebody opened the slide gate between the two chutes and Prime Time moved into the center chute.

"Oh, no!" Donnie protested. "I want Prime Time to buck from the back chute."

"Do you want us to move him?" one of the cowboys asked Donnie.

"Nah, leave him in the middle chute. He'd buck out on a Walmart parking lot," he said. Donnie flanked Prime Time for me.

Before I approached the chute, I resolved that Prime Time would probably have his day and I would have my hands full.

The time finally came. I climbed into the chute and sat on Prime Time, my feet on the rails. I felt anticipation race through me like electricity. I licked my lips, tasting gritty arena dust. As requested, my friend Glenn Sullivan moved into position, ready to pull my rope for me.

First, I heated up the rope using rosin and friction, just like I'd always done. "Give me some slack," I told Glenn. Next, I heated up the handle, stuck my hand in there, and pulled it tight. "A little bit more, Glenn." He got it snug. "That's it." I took my wrap and laid it across my hand. Padded my fist, put my thumb across. Grabbed hold of the gate. Walked my feet forward and scooted to my rope.

Y'all, when I hit my rope, I felt a surge of confidence like I'd never felt in my whole life. "I'm gonna ride this bull!" I told Glenn.

Until I hit that rope I hadn't truly believed I could ride Prime Time. My only thought had been that I'd sure try. Feeling like a little eight-year-old boy again—the one with no rhyme or reason to think he could ride a rank bull—I *knew* I could do it. I felt stuck to my rope.

I heard Randy's voice over the sound system. "Terry, jump for jump, pardner. Prime Time Skoal is the bull. Terry Holland, Panola County, Carthage, Texas."

I took a deep breath and nodded my head. I wanted this final, last-time-in-my-life ride to go on forever. Donnie Gay opened the gate.

Prime Time and I exploded from the chute. His head came right up in my face on the first jump. He turned back and to the left in a spin, but the rest of the ride became a blur. I felt his power, speed, and intensity.

Twenty years of competing had taught me that riding a rank bull is not the time to think. My subconscious kicked in and I rode, my free hand matching Prime Time's every move.

I never heard the whistle signaling the end of eight seconds. I just knew I'd ridden long enough and got off into my hand, rolled midair, and landed on my knees and hands.

After analyzing my ride on video later, I saw exactly what happened. The whole time Prime Time bucked, he never had all four feet on the dirt at the same time. Most of the time, his feet were completely off the ground. He jumped and twisted—his rear end went one direction and his front end another. He planted front feet in the dirt and swung his back end up and around, pivoting and turning to the left as he went. Prime Time continued his awesome, athletic performance, plunging forward, spinning to the left, kicking the dust behind him.

As I hit the ground, Jimmy Anderson, one of the best bull fighters in the business, stepped between me and Prime Time. I jumped up and headed for the arena fence. Over my shoulder I saw Prime Time trotting through the let-out gate to the alley way and stock pens.

Whooping, hollering, and applause burst from the audience.

I turned and walked toward the chute. Donnie Gay gave me a bear hug. I received congratulations, slaps on the back, more hugs, and handshakes from the bull fighters and other cowboys in the arena and around the chutes.

"Great ride," said someone nearby.

"We're gettin' a score now." Randy spoke over the crowd's noise. "I've gotta tell y'all, this is a very special moment for me as well. I didn't say this 'cause I knew I'd get choked up a minute ago. Don knows what I'm about to say.

"Terry knew me as a bull rider several years ago. He gave me an opportunity in Carthage to meet the man you see here, Don Gay. Terry was very instrumental in my career as an announcer. Terry, thank you so very much.

"Gotta score comin' up," Randy said to the audience. "We're gonna give Terry an opportunity to talk to you folks here, and for a good reason. He's one of our own." Randy tossed the microphone down into the arena. "Catch this..."

Donnie handed me the portable mike.

Still breathless from my ride, I waited a moment to speak. "Tell you what, folks. I can't even remember when I didn't want to ride bulls. When I was five years old, I met Jim Shoulders, the greatest cowboy ever. He inspired me, and even at five I knew what I was gonna do. When I was a little boy, I told my teachers that I was gonna ride bulls for a living the rest of my life. Well, the rest of my life is thirty-eight years. I still love to ride bulls, but I love my Lord and Savior, Jesus Christ, more."

The crowd went wild. Several moments later, the noise subsided enough for me to continue.

"I knew this would be tough. Rodeoing is hard on a man—it's a hard life. There are lots of rewards, but it's harder on his wife." I struggled to keep my voice steady. "Tonight, I tip my hat to my wife, Debbie Jo." The applause swelled. "She was with me, encouraging me. She and my little girl, Khakie Jo, have been crying all week wanting me to keep doing it. But I always wanted to quit while I could still ride. I guess I can. I'd like to give the glory to the Lord."

Cheers and whistling rose from the stands.

"The greatest highlight of my rodeo career happened right here in this arena and it wasn't riding that bull. Two years ago, Donnie Gay walked up to me in front of the same bucking chute I just came out of. He told me he'd given his life to Jesus Christ. *That* is the highlight of my career." I handed the mike back to Donnie.

"If we can't cheer a champion, we can't do nothin'," Donnie said. "Folks, let's stand up and cheer Terry Holland. He started the rodeo season this year. Earlier this week, he told us this was gonna be a farewell tour. And, indeed, it's so-long-to-ridin'-'em and what a way to do it. Terry's tonight's *champion* with eighty-nine points!"

There are no great victories without great challenges, and this victory tasted sweet.

I thought it would be nice, when I retired, if people talked about Terry Holland being a great bull rider. Wouldn't that be neat? That's what I wanted—for someone to remember me. If they didn't say "great" maybe they'd at least say "pretty good."

After I rode Prime Time, I thought I'd given folks something to talk about. They'll remember me for doing this. And sure enough, I didn't walk very far before someone said, "What a ride. That was great. Man, Terry, you're the best."

You know, the remark didn't feel as good as I'd expected, because what happened that night wasn't about me. God honored me—not, I believe, for riding bulls twenty years, but for being obedient to him and persistent in my walk with Christ.

Sure, I made mistakes. But I took Jesus Christ with me everywhere I went. I never compromised my faith and continued to serve God no matter what, often in an atmosphere that wasn't conducive to being a Christian. That's why he blessed me and gave me a special night. As I walked away, I thought, *I'm not great at all*. And it felt really good *not* to be. But I knew who was great and still is—my God.

I knew he had written the script and put on the show. He gave me the burning desire to sell those bulls to Don Gay. The whole thing had been orchestrated for a long time. I just fell in there, got on the track, and rode it out. God simply blessed me.

Several months later on the way to San Antonio, I had a revelation about what that night did to me. I'd offered up the best I had—couldn't reach down and get anymore—just offered my absolute very finest. If I could go back and ride bulls again, I'd ride every single one like it was the last. Every ride would be as special as that night in Henderson, because I'd do it the same every time and always offer up my utmost.

I took this thought a little further and decided to live life and love my family with as much passion as I'd ridden my last bull. I didn't realize I could love my family any more than I already did, but that night gave me insight to a new dimension and a deeper awareness than I'd had before. I pursue excellence now in everything I do and because of this, I won't remain the same.

I probably had more great rides in 1980 than any other year. Here I'm winning 2nd at Cheyenne, WY on a Don Hight bull. That's Legendary Hall of Fame bull fighter, Wick Peth, in the background.

Head Knocker was one of the last bulls I got on my final season, 1997. We're at Conroe, Texas in this photo. It certainly made for a wild picture. Photo by Phifer.

I love this picture from Cheyenne in 1982. I didn't win anything with this ride, but you have to admit, it looks good. I rode with three broken ribs I'd gotten the day before in Ogden, Utah. By the end of the week, my lung collapsed. Photo by: Al Long, Granbury, Texas.

A lot of money was always up for grabs at the Houston Rodeo, but over the years all I ever won there was $73 for this ride in 1980 on #250 of Dell Hall's. Photo by: Huffman Foto.

1979. Riding Cervi's #5. At 19 I rode in the Astrodome for the first time in front of a packed house. That was about as good as it could get. Photo by: Huffman Foto.

I rode a lot of bulls at the Mesquite Weekly Rodeo where I earned the respect and friendship of stock contractor, Neal Gay, a man I admire greatly. In this photo, flank-man Pete Gay watches me stick it on G81 Dillinger. Photo by: Kerby.

This wild ride happened in Stephenville, Texas, 1987. After I dismounted, this bull hooked my shirt off. Opening the gate is 1978 World Champion, Butch Kirby. He was absolutely no help during the hooking. Photo by: Dudley Barker, Stephenville, Texas.

I'm riding Cervi's #113 here at one of my favorite rodeos—Sidney, Iowa, in 1980. There was a place in town where the cowboys could eat all the sliced tomatoes and corn on the cob they could stand for free.

I hate this bull! He bucked me off and hooked me every time I got on him. This time was at the Texas State Fair in Dallas, 1979. Photo by Huffman Foto.

Chapter 23

With blocks taped to the clutch and brake, I started running tractors for my dad when I was about nine. My mom objected to my brothers and me working so much so young. I couldn't wait. I liked working with my dad. He and I have spent a lot of time together.

When kids are raised around the farm or ranch, some will love it. I did and Khakie does too. Others will try and get as far away from country life as they can. My two older brothers didn't fall in love with the ranch life or farming. They chose to do something else with their lives.

When I made the decision to remain at the ranch, I ended up spending even more time working with my dad. Honestly, he aggravated me. We didn't see things the same way. I had different ideas on how to work, pen, and sort cattle. He knew I was good at what I did. It was just that the things I accomplished weren't done the same way as he'd have done them. Having my own ideas created a lot of strife between us as I grew up, but the older I became, I pretty much let him do things the way he wanted to.

I think the relationship my dad and I have is special, even though we still don't always see eye to eye. Over the years I've learned his ways, and I know how he operates.

Now, every single morning I go check in with him while he's having his coffee. We discuss what's going to happen that day. The more I'm around my daddy, the more he influences me. I can feel the way he thinks. I know how he feels about any given subject. I know what he wants before he actually says it.

My dad developed a type of sign language for my brothers and me. The noise of our machinery and the distance between us made hand signals useful and necessary for communication. Opening your hands up means leave the gate open. Clapping your hands together means close the gate.

He could look across the field, recognize a problem coming and signal me. His arm waving looked chaotic if you didn't understand him. I felt confident and comfortable around my dad, because I understood his signals and signs.

On those old tractors, to rev them up and go faster, we had to pull down on a little hand throttle. My dad's signal—a pulling down motion, meant gas it or speed up. If he waved his hand, it meant slow down. The signs are similar, and the guys who didn't know him like I did, got his signs all mixed up.

One day a man stopped by my folks' house to see about leasing some land for a natural gas well. This was before cell phones. Mother called my house.

"Your dad's gone. I can't find him. Where do you think he is?"

"I'm not sure, Mother. Which truck's gone?"

"The old red one."

That meant he was doing some kind of work, because he only took his old truck when he was working. He didn't want to dent his new one.

"I remember him saying two or three days ago he needed to cut down a tree that had fallen on a fence. He wanted to tackle the tree and fix the fence. I'll be down there in a minute."

I went to my folks' place, looked in the barn and sure enough, his chain saw was gone, too.

I turned to the man who needed to see my dad. "Go down this county road, take the first turn to the right, when you pass the church, turn left across a cattle guard, he'll be on the right cutting up a tree that fell on the fence row."

"How do you know that?" he asked.

"I just know him." Sure enough, the man went and found my dad precisely where I said he'd be.

I saw the man later and he couldn't believe I'd known that. Neither could my mother, but I can. Had I not been in frequent communication and tuned to his way of thinking, I wouldn't have known his plans. I wouldn't have been able to find him.

The time I spend with my dad each morning is how I look at the fellowship we have with God. My dad loves the part of our day when we just talk. I believe each minute we spend in prayer and studying God's Word blesses him just like it does my dad.

God desires us to stop in and "have coffee" with him every morning. If we read and study his Word, then we'll know what he wants before he tells us. We'll know where he is and how to find him. We'll feel his presence, his way of thinking, and we'll respond appropriately because we've spent time with him.

Debbie Jo and I live in Carthage, but for a time we attended a church in Lufkin. We drove sixty miles each way for services.

One Sunday the pastor announced that the assistant pastor, dying of cancer, had slipped into a coma. "If you want to go see him, you'd better go today because he may be dead by this afternoon," he said.

Something about what he said hit me the wrong way. We went on home after church was over and came back for the six o'clock service that night. After the evening service we started toward Carthage. We rode in silence for miles, but something bugged me.

"Deb, I know he's an old man and extremely sick. But we are supposed to go and pray for him!"

"I feel the same way," she said.

We'd never done anything as bizarre as praying for someone to be cured of cancer. I wasn't raised in a church that believed in touching people and praying for healing. We just didn't do it. We believed whatever happens, happens. We prayed for people from a distance but didn't do anything dramatic.

"He's probably dead by now," I said. We were about twenty miles from home at this point and it was almost nine o'clock. "Debbie Jo, we cannot go home. We're supposed to go. I know we're not really the ones qualified to do this, but for some reason we're supposed to go pray for him."

"I believe we are too, Terry."

We turned around and drove the forty miles back to Lufkin. All the way back to the hospital, Deb read healing scriptures from the Bible. We went over them until we got there.

My thoughts told me, "I'm not capable of doing this—I can't handle this sort of thing. Maybe a broken bone or a case of flu, but this is so serious, I just don't know." Yet in spite of my doubts, I knew God was leading us to pray for this man. We had to be obedient.

By the time we got there, it was quite late. His daughters sat huddled outside his room in tears. We hugged them, and they cried.

"Would it be okay if we go in and pray for your dad?" I asked, just to be sure.

"Yes. That'd be fine," one of the daughters said. "Do you want me to go in with you?"

I thought a moment. "No. That's okay." Many times Jesus didn't want someone present if they didn't have faith.

We walked into the hospital room, just the two of us. He looked so horrible.

"We've waited too long," I said. "He's dead." I looked at him. I've seen cows and other animals die. He was not moving. "Debbie," I whispered. "I think I'll go tell the nurse that..."

From the form on the bed came a single deep, raspy breath.

"I don't see how or why, Deb, but we're the ones who've been chosen to do this." We laid our hands on him and began to pray, speaking the Word over him as we did. *By his stripes we are healed ... where two or more are gathered together.* We didn't pray positive stuff, just spoke God's Word—every healing scripture that came to mind. "Father, heal him. I know he's old. I know he's a godly man, and I think it might be time, but restore him. In Jesus' name."

I don't know how long we prayed. Nothing happened. Except for an occasional sucking breath, he continued to appear dead.

Deb and I looked at each other, looked at the man in a coma, unsure of what to do next. We'd done what we believed God wanted us to do. We felt okay about it and left the room. The daughters still sat there outside his room crying. We let them know we loved and cared for them and asked them to let us know how he does. Then we went home.

We didn't understand it and didn't know much about praying for someone who was so ill, that old, and when it seemed time for them to die. We took comfort in the fact that we did what we were supposed to do.

Tuesday, one of his daughters called to tell us he'd passed away. Deb put the call on speaker-phone so I could hear, too.

What? I don't understand, God, why did you impress upon us to go pray for him? He's obviously dead.

The daughter went on to thank us and asked, "What did y'all pray for him?"

Deb and I looked at each other. The way she said it made me think something had happened to him. *Uh oh, we're in trouble.*

Chapter 24

She didn't wait for an answer. "Let me tell you what happened. Monday morning he was still alive. When we went in he awoke and sat up. He hadn't eaten for several days, but he ate like a starving horse. He talked to us. We hugged, kissed, laughed, and cried. We brought in all the grandkids for him to love on. He pulled each one up on his lap and talked to them. He was clear-headed and sensible. We had a huge party. It was absolutely wonderful! Then, that night he died in his sleep."

God had honored this family. We didn't know it, but they had not been able to tell him goodbye, because he'd gone into the coma before anyone could tell them he was so ill.

We wept. That was the first time I remember God impressing upon us to do anything like this. Apparently, God needed a couple of believers for this one, little bitty thing. Nobody else was in line so God destined Debbie Jo and me to do it.

We prayed for him as God led us so they could have a few more hours to tell their dad and grandpa—a man of God—goodbye. Deb and I believe we were part of God's plan for them. He used us to help them realize he did this for them through and because of prayer.

When my daughter, Khakie Jo, was little, she enjoyed going to the hardware store with me. She loved to play with the bolts, washers, nuts, and various stuff in the bins. On one occasion when Khakie was not quite three, I needed some cement mix and took her along.

Deb and I had often discussed the importance of protecting Khakie. Debbie Jo was especially adamant about not leaving our little girl alone in any store for even a second.

I pulled in and parked at the hardware store in an area where I really wasn't supposed to be. The sign said "no parking" because it was a lane for the forklift to safely come and go with bulky items for customers.

Khakie and I went into the store, and although she immediately eyed the nuts and bolts bin, she stayed by my side instead of going to play. I hadn't yet given her permission to do so, and at her young age, she already understood obedience.

"What do you need?" the sales clerk asked.

"Ten sacks of Sakrete cement mix, and I need..."

"Somebody's truck's in the way," a customer standing by the door interrupted. "Who's drivin' a red and white Ford truck?"

"Me!" I ran to the door.

The man pointed. "He's fixin' to hit it with that forklift."

The forklift, loaded down with metal panels, lumbered toward my truck. The driver obviously couldn't see past his load.

"Khakie, you stand *right* here. I love you. I'll be back." Out the door I ran to save my truck from being demolished.

"She'll be fine." The lady cashier in the store hollered after me.

I felt okay about leaving my daughter there, not scared anyone would steal her. I jumped into my diesel pickup and turned the key. The "wait to start" message glowered at me. I didn't have time to wait. I cranked it anyway and shot forward, I hoped, out of the way. The forklift came within inches of the rear end of my truck, and then the driver saw me.

"Oh no, Terry. I'm sorry." The driver said.

I hopped out of my truck and hollered, "I made it. Everything's okay."

"Man, that was close!" He shifted the forklift into neutral.

"Yeah, it was close."

"What do you need loaded?" he asked.

"I need some cement mix. Uh oh! Khakie!" Several minutes had passed since I'd dashed out of the store. I ran back into the store and found her still standing exactly where I'd left her, feet planted in the same spot. She even faced the same direction.

"I can't believe a child would stand that still," said the cashier. "I even offered to let her go play with the washers and bolts. I know how much she loves it, but she wouldn't move."

When I told her, "Stand here," she stood. Even though her favorite things in the hardware store beckoned from nearby.

Sometime afterward I realized what a great picture Khakie had given me of how my relationship should be with my Heavenly Father. When God tells me to follow him or simply to stand, God expects obedience from me just like I expect obedience from my daughter,.

Oh, she was tempted. The lady at the store told her it was perfectly all right to walk over and play with the bolts until her dad came back.

But Khakie's command had been to stand and wait, so the purpose of keeping her safe would be accomplished. I left her with the promise that I loved her and would return.

We've got to believe Jesus loves us and trust him enough so when he says, "I love you and need you to stand right here," we do it. Because he's also promised to come back for us. When he does, I hope he finds me where I'm supposed to be. Just like Khakie Jo.

"Terry, I know where Prime Time is." Rick, a friend from Arkansas, called me one day almost five years after I'd retired from bull riding. "He's up here, and I can get him for you."

"What do you mean?" I asked.

"The bull can be bought."

"Buy him, please. Whatever it takes. Just buy him."

Donnie had always planned to give Prime Time back to me, but when he sold his rodeo company, Prime Time went with it.

The guy who bought Donnie's business was a logger and treated the rodeo company like the logs he hauled. He would put Prime Time and the other bulls on a truck, take them to rodeos, and buck them. A friend of mine saw Prime Time after Donnie sold the business. The former champion was poor, thin, and pitiful—obviously abused.

Then some other folks bought Prime Time from the rodeo company and put him in the pasture with some cattle.

Around July 4, 2002, I laid eyes on Prime Time for the first time in several years. I happened to be in the area close to where he lived and went by to see him. He looked beautiful—big, good looking, fat, and sleek.

Rick had worked the deal to buy Prime Time and he called. "Terry, you can have this bull the last weekend in September. You come to the ranch and pick him up."

Well, I was going to be in Benton, Arkansas, at a PBR event not far from Rick's ranch.

Rick had him penned, and after I got there I loaded him into my trailer. Prime Time jumped in and turned sideways, ready to hit the road.

I made out the check right then to a man named Johnny Harper. I wrote in his name, the amount, and signed it. I always date my checks last. I wrote the date without thinking. *September 28, 2002.* Then I realized it was five years ago to the day that I rode Prime Time.

Chapter 25

I used to watch the rodeo and bull riding telecasts and think, *I could do that analyst work! I'm a natural for it*. But I never told anyone and I'll tell you why. Announcer gigs are few and far between, and there're only a handful of opportunities to do any work like that on television. You know, it just seemed to be locked up. I put my secret longing aside. My dream seemed impossible and I knew it.

I had been combining a little amateur announcing and analyst work with ministry opportunities. Our friends Bill and Karen Shaw were involved in a rodeo outreach and I helped them out.

About that time Terry Williams, five time PBR stock contractor of the year, came up with a new bull riding organization/association called Championship Bull Riding (CBR). As I drove to judge one of those CBR events, Terry Williams called me. "Do you think you could do that on TV?" he asked.

"What do you mean?" I didn't dare hope.

"Do you think you could do the part where the analyst talks about the ride and looks at the slow motion?"

"Man, I think I can." My heart pounded with excitement.

"Talk to Allan Blakeney tonight when you get to Little Rock. He's the producer of the show. I think I got you the deal. I'll see you later."

I got to Little Rock and started to wonder. *Does this guy even know I'm coming and that I'm supposed to talk to him?* I hunted him up anyway. He seemed to be a little motorcycle rider, a little hippie. He was a long-haired guy with a rag on his head.

"Hi Allan, I'm Terry Holland." I shook his hand.

"Terry Williams said you might come by and talk to me. Do you think you can do this program?"

"I think I can. I've never done anything like it. I'm a Christian motivational speaker and I'm used to speaking a lot in front of large groups."

"Have you ever spoken in front of several million people?"

I shook my head. "No, can't say that I have. If you add 'em all up, maybe a couple thousand."

"Here's what we're going to do..."

He went on and explained how these television shows work. Allan films the bull riding event, takes it to his studio in Monroe, and puts together a one hour show from all the footage he's recorded. He adds commercials, sometimes interviews a cowboy then throws in stats or rodeo trivia to make it more interesting. Because the rodeos take place in various locations all over the country, Allan sometimes highlights local tourist attractions.

The analyst watches the rodeo in the studio on a monitor. He calls the action play by play just like he's at the event seeing it for the first time.

I called Debbie Jo. "You ain't gonna believe this. I'm fixin' to get my chance." I was so excited and crazy. Never did I think I'd actually have this kind of opportunity.

Lord, thank you! You know my desire, and you're letting me have it. I didn't beg anybody—they came to me. Thank you Lord for giving me favor with these people.

I was going to be working alongside Bob Tallman, who's an announcer in the Pro Rodeo Hall of Fame. He's probably the most famous rodeo announcer on the planet. He's done tons of television. He's the best who's ever done it and probably still is. *Man, this is goin' to be lots of pressure.*

I went to the studio and found Andy Stewart, another announcer, working on the show, too. They'd asked me to help because neither he nor Bob really knew bull riding enough to analyze the rides, plus he wanted someone to host the bull riding show. They needed someone who could say, "Here's what's goin' on." That's where I was supposed to fit in.

Bob came in a little late that day. When we finally got started, Allan came in and sat down. "I'm going to be real honest. Terry, I don't know if we can use you or not on The Outdoor Channel. We thought we were going to use just one announcer, but I don't want to lose Andy and Bob is so well-known."

He pulled me over to the side. "I know you came all the way over here. I'll pay you for coming. You can sit and watch us do the three shows we have planned for today, but I can't have three guys—can't afford it. I'm so sorry, I just don't think we can use you."

"Terry Williams said you wanted a bull rider for the show."

"I know it, but we can't afford three announcers," Allan said.

I figured he didn't know for sure if I could do it. My few little speeches here and there didn't mean much to him, and he was afraid to take the chance. He didn't know what I knew or that I'd ridden bulls for twenty years.

Suddenly, it dawned on me. I realized then it wasn't just about money and fitting me into the budget. I figured they thought they'd just see if I was any good—if I messed it up, it's not a big deal, but they'll audition me and see how I do.

"How 'bout this? I'll do these shows today for free. You don't have to pay me anything. If I'm doing terrible, stop me right there before we get goin' and I'll get out of the way. If I do well enough that you want me to keep doin' the shows, then call me when it's time to do some more of them. If I don't ever hear from you, that'll be just fine. I'll be tickled to death that I got to do even a little bit of it."

Allan smiled. "I can do that. Sounds good." Allan motioned to Bob and Andy. "We're giving Terry a try here."

I did the first show, the next, and then the third show. For the first one, I didn't do much. The others took it easy and sort of played like they were bringing in a new guy. They'd ask me to comment on some of the rides. By the second show, I analyzed every single ride by slow motion. So far, Allan hadn't said anything about it not working.

I had a bad habit at the time, which thank goodness, I don't do anymore on television. I'd say, "I'll tell you what..." before I commented. It seemed everybody, not only in East Texas but just about the whole world, preface what they're going to say with "I'll tell you what." So I used it, too. I'd hear it on every ESPN telecast. My whole family and everyone I know says it.

"I'll tell you what, Bob, this bull right here'll turn back and he's pretty rank."

"Tell you what, when this bull turned back to the left, that guy looks a little out of shape."

The producer finally stepped in. "Terry, we've got to do away with that 'I'll tell you what' business."

It was tough, but I got a grip on it.

After the third show, the producer patted me on the back. "Appreciate you, Terry." Allan, Bob, and Andy all told me I'd done a good job.

I suspected they were just trying to encourage me, but I went home thankful for the experience.

About two weeks later the phone rang. "Can you be over here Monday morning at nine?" Allan asked.

"Yep."

Getting Bob there to do the shows became more difficult because of his busy schedule. It ended up with Andy and me doing the bull riding events. The Outdoor Channel fans voted the bull riding show their favorite and awarded us a Golden Moose Award two years in a row, 2004 and 2005.

Some things began changing in the CBR. Tuff Hedeman became their president to help get it jumpstarted. At the live events, they had a segment called "Tuff's Picks" where he'd do clips, interviews, predictions, and comments.

Not long after that started, I could see the writing on the wall. They wanted to replace me with Tuff. My producer, Allan Blakeney didn't want to, but it wasn't up to him, and they let me go.

It broke my heart. I'd worked hard and it just wasn't supposed to happen that way, but I kept my joy and thanked the Lord for letting me have the opportunity even though I was disappointed. I appreciated Terry Williams for giving me the chance.

Before I left the studio, I had to know. "Am I any good at this?" I asked Allan.

Allan nodded. "Terry, you're real good. You're the best we've had on this show. I'm going to try and get you some more work."

"Thanks." We shook hands before I left.

The first bit of work he put me into was Grand Prix jumping horse shows—which I knew nothing about. Allan was so good to me and let me draw a check for doing these horse shows even though I knew so little about them. At first it was tough. Later I grew more comfortable and announced some calf roping events and college rodeos. Allan let me continue working here and there whenever he could.

One day he called. "Terry, we're going to meet with the PRCA. I know you rodeoed in the PRCA for a long time. It looks like The Outdoor Channel will be doing a lot of coverage for their rodeos, and you're going to be their guy."

Of course I was thrilled about it.

They made the deal. The first year we did twenty-six shows. The 2007-2008 expanded and grew to be even bigger.

I'd rodeoed in the PRCA and gained experience along the way. Calling those calf roping events helped make me a better announcer/analyst and taught me about this event. I'd ridden saddle broncs in high school and hung around with numerous champion bronc and bareback riders through the years, so I learned a lot about it even though I didn't do much of it myself. This show required me to have knowledge of *every* event—team roping, steer wrestling, barrel racing, bareback riding, saddle bronc, *and* bull riding. All those experiences from the past helped make me capable of doing rodeo announcing for the PRCA shows.

I got myself a little lesson there in turning loose—letting go of one thing and allowing the Lord to replace it with something else a whole lot better.

Chapter 26

We were working at the Allison place near Fairplay, Texas, worming and vaccinating cows and their calves. Bryan Pride, a friend of mine who's also in the cattle business, had been working his cattle as well.

We'd rounded up most of the cattle and were waiting for Bryan to drop off the cattle de-wormer for us to use. He had connections and could get de-wormer at a discount price. I'd asked him to get me enough to do three hundred cows. Bryan pulled over along the road next to the fence while we finished penning the last few head. I looked up to see him wave at me.

"I'm gonna set it here by the road," he hollered.

"Wait there a minute and I'll pay you for it," I said. To worm that many cows cost around thirteen hundred dollars.

"Don't worry about it. You ain't going nowhere. I'll see you somewhere and you can pay me later."

Bryan set the container out and left. I figured I'd see him in day or two and pay him then.

The next day we heard Bryan had been seriously hurt while working cattle for someone in Louisiana. Bryan had been on horseback pushing cattle into a pen, along with his two young boys and several other cowboys. As they got right up to the gate, one cow broke, turned, and left the rest of the herd. Bryan had rodeoed in high school in the team roping competition. Although they didn't want a cow to breakaway from the herd, knowing Bryan, it was probably perfectly all right with him, because it gave him a chance to run a cow down and rope it. I figured he had his lariat in hand, swinging the loop to push the cattle along.

His rope ready, Bryan took off on horse after this cow to bring her back to the pen. He roped the renegade cow. Just as he tied off to his saddle horn, his horse stumbled and flipped head-over-heels as the other hands, friends, and his boys watched it happen. His head hit the ground so hard it knocked him out cold.

Someone used a cell phone to call for help. While they waited for the helicopter to arrive, Bryan did not regain consciousness and at one point even stopped breathing. Though the adults knew Bryan's injury was serious, they tried to reassure his boys. A little while later a Life Flight helicopter landed in the pasture.

The whole community joined in concern and prayer for Bryan. The accident happened early in the week. By the weekend, he was still unconscious. The word spread and on Sunday local pastors shared the situation in area churches and asked members to pray for Bryan.

I remember hearing the request at my church. Our family had already been praying for him. I felt confident God could heal and restore Bryan as a result of the community's prayers. His situation was serious and the longer it went, the more grim it seemed.

Our pastor wasn't preaching this particular Sunday. Instead, our youth pastor, James Boggs, spoke. I don't recall much about what he preached, just that the Holy Spirit impressed upon me the need to pray for Bryan Pride.

"But I *am* praying for Bryan," I told God.

Whatever James preached on began to prick my heart. I couldn't get away from it. The Lord continued to compel me to go and pray for Bryan *in person* and physically lay hands on him.

Surely, somebody's already done that. With so many people already praying, what difference could it make for one man to go and lay hands on him? Would that make the difference in his being restored and healed? I wondered. I couldn't make the feeling go away.

I tried to blow it off that Sunday. *My prayers and physical presence can't be that important.* Monday it kept working on me. By Tuesday, I almost couldn't stand it anymore.

So I asked the Lord, "What am I supposed to do?" Everytime I asked this question in my prayer time, I knew the answer in my heart. The Lord directed me to go and lay hands on Bryan Pride. He was in intensive care and still in a coma. He hadn't responded; no signs of him coming out of it. His family had become distraught, discouraged, depressed, and tired of bad news. Nothing looked promising.

I was puzzled at why no change came in Bryan's condition, because I knew a whole lot of people were praying for him.

I continued to feel God's urging to go in person and pray. *Maybe that's what I need to do.* It seemed whenever I decided to go would be the right time, and it didn't feel like I wasn't getting there soon enough.

On Tuesday Allan Blakeney, the rodeo program producer, called and asked me to be at the studio in Monroe, Louisiana, by nine o'clock Wednesday morning for a broadcast. From Carthage, it's about a two and a half hour trip. I'd be driving right through Shreveport on the way to Monroe. Bryan was in ICU at LSU Medical Center in Shreveport, Louisiana.

As I left early the next morning, I said to myself, "If it all works out just right, I'm gonna stop by and pray for Bryan." After doing the show I headed for home. As I drove toward Shreveport, I began to pray and meditate on God's Word and any scriptures I could recall that had to do with healing. I arrived in Shreveport hungry, a little nervous, and not quite ready to head to intensive care. First, I'd have to ask the family to somehow get me in to see Bryan, then I'd pray for him. I didn't know how this was going to work out.

I stopped at El Chico's, read my Bible, studied, and got myself prayed up while I ate lunch. It seemed as though I was stalling, but really, I wasn't. Finally, I headed over to the medical center and parked.

Before I left my truck I said, "Lord, I want to please you. I know you're requiring me to go in person and pray for Bryan. Father, I'm gonna be obedient. You've blessed me with so much; I bless you back by going in here. I'm not a pastor. I don't have a healing ministry. I don't know how you can use me—I'm just an old cowboy rancher like Bryan—but I love Jesus."

I went in to the ICU waiting area. Bryan's family had gathered with friends and folks from their church. I arrived during regular ICU visiting hours. Bryan's wife, Anissa, and his dad were in by his bedside.

"Howdy. How's Bryan?" I asked his mom in the waiting room. She looked glad to see me in spite of her discouragement. "Would it be possible to go in and see him?"

"Come on, Terry. You can see him right now," she said. She grabbed my arm and led me down the hall past room after open room of really ill people.

We came to Bryan's space where Anissa held his hand. "Baby, I love you," she said. "You're gonna be just fine." She told him what had been going on with their kids.

I walked over. "I just wanted to come and see Bryan. I believe the Lord wants me to pray for him. Is that okay?"

"Well, sure. That'd be great," Anissa said.

ICU limits the number of people in the room to two at a time. Bryan's parents left. Anissa stayed with me.

Bryan looked terrible—all swollen, with tubes running everywhere, machines breathing for him. I was in over my head, but I felt confident Bryan was supposed to recover and complete some purpose in his life. I looked down at him. *This boy don't look good. He looks nearly dead.*

I turned to Anissa. "I'm certainly not capable of restoring his health, but my God is! We have to see this as he sees it, not as it looks to us. I feel the Holy Spirit instructed me to come here because God's not through with Bryan."

Anissa bowed her head and closed her eyes.

I put my hands on Bryan's shoulder and began to pray. "Lord, because of Jesus Christ and what he did, I pray for Bryan Pride's healing. Lord, make Bryan whole again and able to do any and every thing he's ever done just as he was before the accident. I thank you, Lord, and ask by faith in Jesus Christ." I spoke scripture over him and repeated my prayer for restoration and wholeness. I finished, "In Jesus' name. Amen."

Well, I'd done what I was supposed to do, so I opened my eyes. *He may be fixin' to jump up right now.* I got ready, expecting it to happen immediately. I had such faith in God's power and in what he'd told me to do, I knew Bryan would be restored.

Anissa stood by the bed looking down at him, her physical and emotional exhaustion obvious. "Thank you, Terry." Tears ran down her cheeks. "It means a lot to have you stop by."

We turned to go and took a couple steps away. "See you later, Bryan," I said. Something stopped me. "I'm not through." I turned back, but Anissa kept walking. I leaned close to Bryan's face.

He used to do an interesting trick—he could fold his ear up, real quick, turn it underneath and lap one part over like you'd fold up a triangular paper football.

I chuckled as I thought about it and bent down close to his ear. "Bryan, it's time you showed your family a good sign. They need to see something positive. They need a sign from you, Bryan. You can do it. In the name of Jesus, give them some hope!" Now, it felt like I was done.

Back in the ICU waiting room folks laughed and cried together. I told stories about Bryan's dad, who was maybe ten years older than me, driving fast and spinning out, pulling onto the highway beside our house.

Finally, I started toward Marshall to pick up several of my Mighty Bucky products from the upholstery shop before I went home. I felt spiritually exhausted, physically thirsty, and decided I needed a snack. I took the Carthage exit off Interstate 20 about fifteen miles from the hospital. After I stopped at Arby's for a drink and apple pie, I got back on the interstate. My cell phone rang. I glanced at the screen, but didn't recognize the number.

"Hello?"

I heard a woman's sobs.

Alarmed, I pulled over onto the shoulder so I could concentrate. "Hello? Hello?"

Chapter 27

The voice finally answered. "Terry, this is Anissa."

Fear leapt into my heart. Now I was really scared and upset.

She stammered, trying to talk, her voice smothered by tears. Anissa got out a few words. "I just left Bryan. He... he gave us a sign!"

"What'd he do?" It couldn't have been more than an hour since I'd prayed for him and left the hospital.

Anissa regained some of her composure. After I left, Bryan's doctors and family had gone into the room.

"Bryan, if you can hear us, raise your hand,'" one of them said, like they had several times before. For the first time, he did as asked. "Bryan, hold up a finger," another doctor said. Bryan did. The doctors didn't seem too impressed.

Listening to Anissa tell what had happened brought tears to my eyes.

Anissa wanted to test him even further. "'Bryan, if you can hear me, hold up two fingers.' He stuck two fingers in the air! 'If you can hear me, give me a thumbs up.' He held up his hand, thumb in the air."

Right there on the side of the interstate I praised God for what he'd done.

The next day I drove back, went into his hospital room, and prayed for him again. This time while I prayed for Bryan, he opened his eyes and blinked, then closed them again. He wasn't focused on me or looking around the room, but it was a huge improvement over the way he'd looked when I first saw him.

Bryan's family thanked me repeatedly. "It's not me," I said. "Just thank God! God has shown himself real to y'all. Praise and thank him. You've seen a miracle."

Bible in hand, I left the ICU and walked out the hospital's busy front door. A lot of people sat around the entrance area, some smoking cigarettes. The Lord told me once I saw Bryan's recovery for myself, there was something

else He wanted me to do—pray in public at the front of the
hospital on my knees where I could see the LSU Medical
Center sign.

I thought it seemed kind of weird, but God had made it
clear that's what I was supposed do. After I noticed how
many people were hanging around the entrance, it got to
working on me.

*I'll just get over here beside this tree. I can sort of see the
sign and the hospital entrance, and I won't stick out so
much.* My thoughts reminded me that I'd experienced God's
power—I'd seen a miracle.

"Ah, shoot," I said. "I'm gonna do it just like you told me
to." I walked on past all those people to a grassy area right in
front of the entrance and the sign. I got down on my knees,
took off my cowboy hat, and holding my hands out began to
praise God and pray. Oh, I could feel people looking at me
and knew they wondered why I was doing that. I didn't stay
there a long time, but just thanked him for what he'd shown
me. I thanked him for asking me, for using me, for letting
me be a part of his plan. He gave me the honor of being the
one he sent. The fact that God could use a cowboy like me—a
common person, not a pastor or evangelist—just someone
who knows Jesus, awed me. I thanked him that I'd listened
and had been obedient.

I got to my feet, and sure enough, there *were* a lot of
people looking at me. I put my cowboy hat back on. Well, I
thought, they probably think I'm weird. And it *is* a little
strange the way things seem to work in our world, but I felt
at peace.

Bryan continued to improve and came out of the coma,
even though he stayed in the hospital for quite awhile. He
began to recognize people. He played with his children. I
suspect learning to walk and talk again was one of his
biggest challenges.

One evening in the middle of May I saw Bryan at the
Carthage Professional Rodeo. He sat in a box seat dressed in
his cowboy clothes. He'd lost a lot of weight and wasn't quite
himself yet, but I *knew* he would be completely restored. All
through this, the Lord told me Bryan would be just like he
was before the accident. One day he'd be able to do his ranch
work, just like he did before his injury.

Early that fall while working in a pasture with my backhoe, I looked up and saw a pickup coming toward me. When it got close, I realized who it was. *Golly, Bryan Pride is driving a truck*! I hadn't seen him for a couple of months.

"Hey, Terry. I'm stuck down here mowing in my pasture. Can you come pull me out?" Bryan asked.

"Man, I'd love to. Where're you at?"

He told me his location and headed on back.

I drove the backhoe to the spot. Extending the hoe on the boom, I pulled the tractor out and got him on high ground.

Bryan's a man of few words. "Thank you, Terry," he said.

"All right, man. No problem. If you need me, you know where I am." I gave it some throttle and started back toward my pasture.

I glanced around and saw Bryan turn and come back toward me. I stopped and jumped down from my seat.

"Terry, uh, ah, I just, I just wanted to tell you that, uh, I appreciate you for comin' and prayin' for me that day when you did. I, 'preciate ya for it. And I just wanted to tell you that."

"Bryan, you're welcome," I said.

He got on his tractor, and I climbed up onto my backhoe. We both went back to work. That was more than a couple of years ago. He's working cattle now. Totally restored. Every time I see Bryan Pride, I thank God for asking me and I thank him that I responded with obedience.

Allan Blakeney, along with his wife Rebecca, produce the Professional Rodeo television show for the Outdoor Channel that I add the commentary to. First, he or sometimes Rebecca goes with the crew and films the rodeos. They record each event from various camera angles and take it back to the studio where Allan selects footage from the different shots, edits the film, inserts advertisements in the right spots, and "builds" the shows. I come in later and record my analysis of the events. Allan combines my voice-over recording with the edited film to produce a seamless show.

I work with him a lot in the studio, see both of them at events, and have spent many hours in their home. Allan and

Rebecca have become close friends of mine. They're good people and treat me great.

Usually, we built the shows at Allan's studio in Louisiana. But during the summer of 2007, we flew to Temecula, California, every other week and put things together there. Because Allan's crew filmed so many rodeos in such diverse locations and were on the road so much, they couldn't get back home to Louisiana in time to build the shows before they aired. So they'd overnight the material to the Outdoor Channel studio in Temecula, and then I'd fly out and record the voice-over commentaries on the weekend. Many times Allan flew out, too.

On one particular trip to California, I met Allan at DFW where we were catching the same plane. Allan looked awful.

"Hey, what's the matter?" I asked him.

"My stomach. Something's not working right. I feel terrible."

"You shouldn't have come out here," I said.

He sighed and set down his bag. "I think I can make it."

The flight didn't improve his discomfort. We checked into the hotel and Allan went straight to his room.

I'd had trouble with ulcerative colitis in the past and tried to think of something that might help him. Nothing I came up with seemed to work.

The next morning, Allan couldn't even get out of bed. He told all of us in the crew to go ahead without him. We knew something had to be seriously wrong because Allan loves doing these shows. Dedicated, talented, and professional, Allan knows how he wants them done, but that day there was no way he could oversee the process.

We had planned to edit the film footage, record the voice-over, let Allan rest up and get to feeling better, then catch the red eye flight back to Louisiana—he on to Monroe, me to Shreveport. The crew and I checked on him periodically through the day, but he didn't improve at all. When anyone mentioned going to a local hospital, he refused.

Allan was in tremendous pain and became dehydrated, because liquid of any kind came right back up. He hadn't eaten anything for several days that stayed down either. I thought Allan looked like he wanted to roll over and die. As my concern for him grew, I called Debbie Jo.

"Have you prayed for him?" she asked.

"I've been thinking about it. I know I need to. I think I'll go down there right now and do it."

"So, go pray for him," she said.

I didn't know how he'd take my praying for him, but figured, *oh well, what can he do?* He wasn't in any shape to do anything or protest, even if he wanted to. I went to his room, talked to him a little bit, and worked up my courage.

"Allan, if it's okay with you, I'm goin' to pray for you," I said.

"Whatever." He was in such misery, he didn't care either way.

"Lord, whatever it takes, use the doctors or just heal and restore him right here so he's able to pursue his life's purpose and fulfill his purpose for you."

He didn't say anything in response, so I wasn't sure how he felt about it.

I never recalled hearing Allan or Rebecca say anything about where they stand—whether or not they're Christians. I just had a feeling they might not be.

Allan still felt terrible, but I helped him into the car we rented for the fifty-mile drive back to the airport. As we headed out, my thoughts told me he should probably go to a hospital in California. When I mentioned it, Allan shook his head. "Not here. My doctor at home knows all about me."

I realized he feared getting stuck in a hospital miles from home.

After turning in the rental, Allan struggled as we walked to catch the shuttle. "Man, we've got a lot ahead of us to get where we need to be. I don't know how I'm going to make it."

"Well, you're just gonna have to," I said.

"I may need some more of those prayers," he said. "If you'll pray for me some more I might can do it."

Well, Lord, he's open and is okay with me praying for him. He didn't think it was goofy. So I prayed for him again.

I figured if we could just get on the flight to Houston and catch our connection to Shreveport, we'd be okay.

I hadn't talked about it a lot, but Allan and the crew knew where I stood—they knew I was a Christian. I'd never shared with him how I came to know Christ. I had thought of this opportunity as only a unique way to use my knowledge, but I began to wonder, what's the real purpose? Is it more than just God giving me the desires of my heart and letting me do what I always wanted to do—be an analyst on television? Then I realized this situation is a little about me and a lot about God blessing me by giving me this chance.

I always hope in whatever I do that I'll impact someone's life in a positive way for Christ. I'd been thinking for a while that Allan needed to hear my testimony. I thought maybe I'd have him and the crew come to one of my speaking engagements and professionally film it. Not only would I get a quality taping for my use, Allan and the rest of them would hear the gospel. But I just hadn't gotten around to doing it yet.

We sat to wait for the plane—Allan on one side of me and a stranger on the other.

The stranger noticed I was wearing one of my sponsorship shirts with Resistol on it. "Are you a bull rider or something?" he asked.

"A *retired* bull rider. We're out here doin' a television show. We put together telecasts of PRCA rodeos on the Outdoor Channel."

"What else do you do?" he asked.

"I raise cattle on a ranch in East Texas," I said. "What do you do?"

"I teach in a Christian school."

He talked about his kids and we enjoyed visiting together.

"How long have you been a Christian?" I asked.

"I became a Christian when I was just a child. I grew up in a Christian family and that's my story. I never did anything really bad."

I knew Allan felt terrible, but I also knew he was listening. Sitting just eighteen inches away from me he couldn't help hearing it, so I shared my testimony with this man.

"I was raised in a Christian home, too. I heard an evangelist on the radio explain salvation. He said I had to make a decision for myself on my own. He explained the only way to God and heaven is through Jesus Christ. This voice on the radio said 'Jesus is the Son of God. He died on a cross and rose from the dead. You must believe that he died on that cross for your sins.'"

I explained what had happened in my life to this stranger, this Christian brother, who really didn't need me witnessing to him at all.

God, you are so cool to have us "randomly" sit down beside this guy who wants to talk about how to know Jesus Christ!

I understood Allan might not hold onto much of what we'd said because of how bad he felt. God gave me the opportunity to share my faith with him through a conversation with someone else, and I knew he would somehow use it for his purpose.

Allan's wife, Rebecca, had to stay in Cheyenne, Wyoming, with the film crew even though she was worried sick about Allan and wanted to be there to look after him.

Instead of continuing on to Monroe, we decided Allan would get off in Shreveport and have his parents drive from Monroe to meet us at the airport. Plus, he'd be with me the whole time on the way home instead of by himself. He stumbled and nearly fell. I half-dragged, half-carried him through the terminal.

"Y'all need to get goin'," I told his folks. Although it was out of character for our relationship, I gave Allan a hug. "Allan, I love you."

He hugged me back like a kid hugging his mama. "I love you, too, Terry."

"You're gonna be all right. I'll be checkin' on you."

They took Allan straight to his doctor's office. After some testing, he discovered Allan had a non-cancerous growth the size of an orange blocking his intestine. It didn't take long after surgery for Allan to feel lots better.

A couple of months later I went over to Allan and Rebecca's house. I noticed her limping.

"You'd better get those lace-ups back on that ankle," Allan told her.

"Rebecca, how'd you hurt your ankle?" I asked.

She smiled. "Well, Terry, I stepped on a rock in the parking lot and twisted my ankle. The first Sunday Allan was able to ride in a car, we went to church."

Chapter 28

Prime Time lives on my ranch now and we pamper him. He's retired from rodeo and has his own pasture. When he's not relaxing in his pasture, he's with a bunch of our cows, hopefully breeding more champion bucking stock.

Even though he's retired, he remembers. Not long ago I was getting ready to load up a few bulls to take to a local bull riding school. Prime Time stood, raised his head, and looked at me.

I opened the trailer door. "Load up if you wanna go."

Into the trailer he went. He moved to the front and turned sideways. I took him along with the others and off loaded them into a pen at the arena. Later in the day, I opened the gate to the alley leading to the chute. Prime Time eased through and made a beeline for the bucking chute, turning his head slightly sideways to keep his horns from bumping the rails on his way through. He didn't hesitate or balk like many of the other bulls. As if he were Mr. Universe on stage, Prime Time flexed his muscles, filling the entire chute.

Because he's retired, I don't buck him anymore, but I invited a few special people to climb into the chute one at a time and take a turn sitting on him for a few moments. After they sat on his massive back, they climbed down and I opened the gate.

Prime Time lunged from the chute and cleared the arena as cowboys and bull fighters all hit the fence. He made his way around the arena tossing his head as he went. Prime Time stopped at the far side near the fence, dipped a horn into the dirt and pawed the ground, sending billows of dust into the air.

Prime Time definitely remembers.

I'm telling you, do you think God isn't good, that he's not for real, and he doesn't care about what you care about? *I* know he does and so does my favorite bull.

Terry and Debbie Jo with one of their Mighty Bucky models.

I brought retired Prime Time to my arena and let him run through the chute and into the arena just for fun.

Glossary

AI (artificial insemination): Injecting sperm into a cow to cause her to become pregnant without the participation of a live bull.

Away from or **into your hand**: Your "hand" refers to whether you ride holding the bull rope in your left or right hand. For example, if a cowboy rides with his left, the handhold is gripped with the left hand and when dismounting "into his hand," he bails off on the left side of the bull. If dismounting "away from his hand," he would bail off on the right side.

Banana horns: Gray colored and hard like regular horns, but have no base so they hang down and flop. They look like two loose bananas swinging from the bull's head Also called scurs. If cattle without horns are crossed with horned breeds, sometimes the result is something in between.

Breeds of cattle: Limousine, Braford, Semintal, Charlois, Brahman, Angus, Hereford, etc.

Brindle: A common color pattern in Brahman-cross cattle; also called tiger-striped.

Bucking into my hand: When a bull bucks and/or spins in the direction of the rider's hand that's holding onto the handhold.

Bull fighter/rodeo clown: His job is to protect bull riders. The term *Rodeo Clown* was used during the 1960s. *Bull Fighter* began being used in the 1970s and is the current term.

Bull names and numbers: Bulls are identified by number brands. Some have names along with the numbers and some don't.

Bull rope: A plaited, loose rope, fourteen to sixteen feet in total length. At its center a leather handhold is braided into the rope and attached to a larger piece of braided poly rope. This rope is strapped around the bull's girth and positioned behind his front legs which puts the handhold in place on his back. The rope is looped and tied so when someone other than the rider pulls it, he can tighten or loosen the handhold for the rider.

Crossbred bull: A combination of two purebred breeds of cattle. For example a Braford is *Bra*hman and Here*ford.*

CBR: Championship Bull Riding. An organization for bull riders.

Cowboy Up: Be tough, ride whether or not you're hurt, or to stop complaining.

Flank strap: Goes around the bull's flank—the area between its back rib and hip. It's similar to the belt a weight lifter wears. It provides support for the bull to push against during the athletic activity of bucking and spinning.

Flank a bull or flanking for a rider: To secure the flank strap around the bull before he leaves the chute.

Fill my permit: In bull riding, winning a thousand dollars in PRCA sponsored competition is called "filling the permit." While earning the required amount toward membership, a competitor participates under a permit, which after it's "filled" allows a participant to apply for membership and buy his card.

Heat up the rope: Using rosin, the rope is rubbed with gloved hands to create friction which makes the rope sticky and creates a better grip.

Lane Frost: World Champion Bull Rider in 1987, Lane was killed in 1989 by a bull while competing in Cheyenne, Wyoming. The movie *Eight Seconds* is about him.

Muley: A bull without any horns.

National Finals (NFR): The National Finals Rodeo includes the top fifteen money-winning contestants from each rodeo event at the end of the season. NFR takes place in Las Vegas, Nevada and includes ten performance finals.

PBR: Professional Bull Riders, an organization for bull riders that promotes the sport.

Polled cattle: Cows without horns.

PRCA: Professional Rodeo Cowboys Association. What became the PRCA was organized initially as a union for cowboys in 1936. Several years and a couple of name changes later, the PRCA (so named in 1975) is the most well-known and oldest organization promoting cowboys and rodeo.

Pull my rope: When a rider's bull rope is tightened with someone's assistance.

Rank: Difficult to ride; very athletic.

Re-ride: If determined by the judges that the bull's performance was substandard, the contestant is given another opportunity to ride a pre-designated animal.

Rigging bag: Cowboy luggage used to transport bull riding equipment.

Scoring in bull riding: A bull ride is judged on a hundred point scale. There are two judges, each with fifty points to disperse. One to twenty-five points for the rider and one to twenty-five for the bull. The bull and rider scores are added together for the total. Even if a rider gets thrown and doesn't make the eight second bell or receive a score, the bull does. This score is used for future rodeo competitions.

Scurs: Also known as banana horns.

Short round: A final round of competition.

Standings: Ranking of contestants by points accumulated or total money won in competition.

Take a wrap: Wrapping the bull rope around the rider's hand and back across it to make a close-fisted grip.

Tiger-striped: Brindle color pattern on cattle.

Turn out/turn out fine: When a contestant decides not to ride the bull he's drawn, it's called "turning out" the bull. There's a twenty-five dollar fee levied if he calls in and notifies the rodeo secretary in advance. If a cowboy simply doesn't show up and doesn't call, there's also a fine involved.

Visible Injury Release: A rodeo contestant is examined by a judge who determines if an injury is sufficient to hamper participation in the event for that night's performance. The contestant pays the fee but there is not a fine added for not participating.

LaVergne, TN USA
06 July 2010
188455LV00001B/5/P